Hope Is Not
A Strategy

Hope Is Not A Strategy

The 6 Keys to Winning the Complex Sale

A simplified, six-step process to manage competitive
sales and prepare your sales team for the new millenium

Proven by world-class sales and consulting organizations

Rick Page

McGraw-Hill

New York   Chicago   San Francisco   Lisbon   London   Madrid
Mexico City   Milan   New Delhi   San Juan   Seoul
Singapore   Sydney   Toronto

The *McGraw·Hill* Companies

20 21 22 23 24 25 DOC/DOC 1 5 4 3 2 1 0

ISBN 0-07-141871-7

McGraw-Hill books are available at special quantity discounts to use as premiums and sales promotions, or for use in corporate training programs. For more information, please write to the Director of Special Sales, Professional Publishing, McGraw-Hill, Two Penn Plaza, New York, NY 10121-2298. Or contact your local bookstore.

DEDICATION

To our customers and sponsors
who trust us all enough to buy from us again and again.

To the many great salespeople and consultants
from whom we have learned.

To the principals and founders of TCS:
Brad Childress, John Geraci, Rob Goodwin, John Hille,
Phil Johnson, Liz McCune, Kathy Millen, Rick Nichols,
Joe Southworth, David Stargel, and Joe Terry.

To Hosea Parker, my father-in-law,
one of the most trustworthy salesmen I have known.

TABLE OF CONTENTS

Section 3: Strategies for Execution

Section 4: Winning Before the Battle— Account Management

ACKNOWLEDGEMENTS

Thanks to the many people who have made this book and our company possible:

Don House, Bill Graves and John Imlay—for getting me started in high-tech selling at MSA.

Contributors and Editors:

Char Baxter – CBC Communications
Klaus Besier – CEO FirePond, formerly CEO SAP America
Dick Biggs – B.O.L.D. Consulting
Peter Bourke – President Spherion, formerly, TCS, Andersen Consulting, IBM
Charles Buffington – C.W. Buffington & Assoc., formerly VP Bellsouth
Mike Coleman – CBC Communications
Jim Costello – VP Carlson Marketing
Ed Cowsar – EVP Novoforum, D&B, TCS, i2
John Demetra – Partner, Deloitte Consulting
Paul DiGiammarino
Bob Fletcher – VP iFleet
John Geraci – COO IMI, formerly TCS, Blessing-White, D&B Software
Rusty Gordon – CEO iFleet
Pat Gross – AMS Founder, Chairman - Executive Committee
Marly Heidkamp – Senior Manager, Arthur Andersen
Tom Kosnik – Consulting Professor, Stanford University
Jack Lane – VP Sales Transchannel, formerly, Andersen Consulting, TCS, DCA, IBM
Ray Lane – Partner, Kleimer, Perkins, Caufield & Byers; former COO of Oracle
Doug MacIntyre – Formerly CEO Firstwave, D&B Software, Infinium
Bruce McCalley – The McCalley Group, formerly Exactium, Datalogix, D&B
Beverly McDonald – President, Socket PR
Tom McNeight – COO Internet Security Systems, formerly D&B Software, Aurum
Karen Neely-Jones – VP Cisco, formerly Oracle, Interim, Wang
Pam Page
Rusty Page – Former VP Sales, NASDAQ
Ryan Parker – Account Manager, Navision
Neal Reynolds – CEO, The Ad Shop
Tom Skelton – Director and former COO, Manugistics
Betsy Walker
Ed Wertzberger – Managing Partner, Arthur Andersen

INTRODUCTION

Why This Book Is Different

When I was a sales manager, I read a book on selling strategically. It said you should have a strategy—but it didn't give you any.

There have been good books on consultative selling—but they ignored competition. There were courses on competitive and political selling that ignored solutions to the business problem—as if you could ignore benefits and win on politics alone.

Hope Is Not A Strategy: Winning the Complex Sale fills the gaps and goes beyond for the first time. It incorporates the best practices from successful practitioners in the areas of *consultative, competitive, political,* and *team selling* into a single, simple, strategic process for winning sales and dominating accounts.

Although much attention is now being focused on client relationship management (CRM), you have to penetrate an account before you can manage it, and many existing accounts still remain competitive. This book primarily addresses the "opportunity" management process of direct business-to-business selling of major commitments. It focuses on developing sales strategies for *teams selling solutions to multiple buyers in competitive evaluations.* The last section addresses how to use proactive account management to win evaluations before they begin or how to avoid them altogether.

In addition, it addresses *new* concepts such as time-based sales strategy for changing issues, effective team-selling talent structures, and a dynamic, four-level strategy process for market, account, opportunity, and individual selling.

This book will take your sales force to the next level.

About the Stories

One of the things our clients at The Complex Sale (TCS) like most about our material is its ability to illustrate our process with anecdotes from our own experience as salespeople and sales managers, and from the experience of our clients at TCS. These stories help relate concepts to real-world experience and make ideas come alive in the mind's eye.

But they must be taken the right way. *Look for the universal teaching point and disregard the details of time, industry, or geography that may not be exactly like you.* This process has been successfully used in the information technology, consulting, medical, telecommunications, and finance industries in many different countries. Parts of the process can be used successfully for other industries.

We have shaded the sales stories and put the historical strategy examples in call-outs with a military icon so readers can skip or explore as their interest leads them. We have also included a brief summary at the end of each of the six chapters that specifically address the keys to the complex sale; those chapters are the heart of the process.

For Consultants

For consultants, we know that the sales model for intangible services is different from that for products—so much so that we pioneered a separate version of our process for professional services firms. We also recognize that for many industries, the term for salesperson is business developer or partner, a customer is a client, and a sale is an engagement. But for the purposes of this book and its general audience, we use the term salesperson.

A book itself is not a solution but the seed of one. A book only creates or confirms awareness. A common sales process and language for an entire enterprise must be installed, customized, and reinforced into the culture by management and delivered by industry sales executives who are respected by their audience. Competitive advantage comes from training and execution that makes a habit of this process.

About the Title

I believe that hope, along with faith and love, are essential to life. Hope is what you do when you have no control. But a strategy is made up of actions and tactics that convert visions to results for those that can make things happen. The title of this book was chosen to accentuate the difference between positive attitudes and positive actions and the flaw of counting on one without the other.

The Challenge— The Complex Sale

CHAPTER 1

Out of Control

Things were going fine in this sale at the beginning but now you feel something's not right. The prospect didn't call back for three days and then suddenly came up with a new requirement—one you can't meet. There's a new person on the evaluation committee you don't know. And you've just discovered that of the two people on the committee who seemed to like you, one is helping the competition and the other is not respected within the company.

The capabilities presentation was uncoordinated and unfocused, and you spent too much time on the wrong topics. Countless hours have been spent coming up with a proposal and the executives are still not accessible. Nothing seems to be driving the prospect to a final decision, but the client is asking for a discount. This deal is out of control.

Many more prospects like this in the forecast and you'll have to tell the CEO a bad quarter is on the horizon. Or that you'll have consultants on the bench with nothing to do. And to make matters worse, your account manager has forecast this business for the current quarter.

Once again, overoptimism has overcome critical thinking.

Hope is not a strategy.

A meteor shower of change is hitting the world of selling, and many salespeople find themselves and their deals spinning out of control.

In the last ten years, the art and science of selling have evolved through several generations, from moving commodities to selling strategic solutions to business partnerships. Unfortunately, some salespeople and managers don't change. They are sales dinosaurs—an endangered species.

The models of buyer-seller relationships are changing rapidly, with the latest impacts coming from five major selling transformations:

1. *Product commodification.* The shrinking half-life of technology means that the window of competitive advantage for products is getting narrower. This means that differentiation often lies in the extended solution, including services, integration, partnerships, supply chain, financing—or trust.

2. *Disintermediation.* The disappearance of the traditional middleman is a result of commodity buyers focusing on driving costs out of the entire supply chain. But some types of buyers still recognize and pay for value. Which strategy do we employ? The answer lies in a sales model for selling the way each customer buys.

3. *e-Commerce.* The Internet will eliminate some salespeople and change others. For repeat orders and products where clients can understand the benefits of the product and configure the order themselves, the Internet will replace the salesperson. Whether they then move to more productive tasks of winning competitive business or helping the clients manage more complex solutions depends on how well the salesperson can learn to add new kinds of value. It's *grow* or *go.*

4. *Customer relationship management.* A system is not a strategy either. Although effective in the customer service area, there is a high failure rate of sales force automation systems among field sales forces. The missing link between a repository of customer information and competitive advantage is a sales *process* that prompts the salesperson for the political, competitive, and consultative information early enough to drive an account strat-

egy that leads to trust in our company, our products or services, and our people.

5. *Business partnering.* There are two types of business partnering. One is teaming with other firms to provide an integrated solution. The other is teaming with clients to solve problems for their customers or constituents. Both mean new sales models for new ways of doing business where the common foundations are shared rewards and trust.

The evolutionary changes facing today's salespeople mean reengineering personal careers so they can bring greater value to their clients. For individuals, this means personal growth and development from often coercive relationships with customers, to collaborative problem solving, to helping clients co-manage their business. For sales managers, it means restructuring sales teams and account strategies. For CEOs, it means changing sales models and messages to new industry markets, competitors, and technology. For consulting partners, it means more proactive ethical competition for fewer high-value accounts. What is actually happening now is computerized relationship management.

You need to move your strategies to the next level, your client relationship to the next level, and yourself to the next level of sales competency.

The salesperson today who thinks he or she is through learning, is through. Look for their footprints in the shale.

The Impact of Change

Today's complex sale encompasses more than just multiple buyers. In the last ten years, the traditional definition of the complex sale has exploded to include new challenges that are overwhelming those salespeople and managers—unless they have a plan to simplify the process.

Buyer preferences for integrated solutions, rather than products, require teams of multiple sellers both inside and outside the vendor organization to help clients discern benefits and differences in complex products or services. Multidepartmental buying committees create shifting requirements and politics in ever-changing competitive evaluations, the primary focus of this book.

Failing to understand and adapt to the immense changes in the buying and selling processes of today results in out-of-control sales situations that experienced sales managers and consulting partners over the years have painfully learned to recognize:

Not returning phone calls. They used to call you back in two hours. Now it's two days. And when they do call you back, their voice is now chilled and formal. Of course, the worst is pure silence: Someone who was planning to buy from you would be asking more questions.

No access to power. You suggest, "My boss will be in town next week to meet your boss. Can we arrange that meeting?" "No, I don't think that will be necessary," is your contact's response. Clients who are thinking about buying from you would probably jump at the chance for managers to meet. Bottom-up selling is the hard road.

New requirement late in the buying process. Suddenly, a new issue appears in the evaluation process. A requirement you can't meet. Where do you think it came from? It came from the competition. You are now on their agenda. Do you think the client is asking you for this response to help you *get* the business? The veteran salesperson knows better. All the client is doing at this point is putting the logical justification on the emotional decision not to buy from you.

Of course, the rookie salesperson, wanting to be responsive to the client, dashes back to the office and cranks out a twenty-page response to the client's request, not realizing that is simply giving the client the bullets with which to shoot you.

Analysis paralysis. The client evaluates and evaluates but doesn't move forward to a decision. And you are running out of things to do. You've sent them the literature and done a presentation, a technical review, and an executive-level overview. You've also had a visit to the client site and corporate headquarters, and yet they appear no closer to purchasing than when you started.

This baffles many salespeople and especially sales managers, but the answer is actually quite clear. There is nobody powerful enough pushing the evaluation to a conclusion, or no business problem painful and urgent enough to cause it to happen. *If business pain or political power for sponsorship is missing from the evaluation, it will sit on your forecast forever.* Unfortunately, the sales manager will probably go away before the deal does.

Rosy forecasts. Some salespeople don't want to ask the tough qualifying questions because it will spoil a perfectly good forecast. The account sits on the forecast and it looks good…until disaster strikes.

Blind spots. Missing information or assumptions about issues, competition, or politics usually end up on a lost sales report. The best salespeople are often the best detectives. They ask the right questions earlier than their competition.

Selling to unqualified prospects. Picking the right battles is the key to resource allocation. Most salespeople in the complex sale work, at most, ten to twenty opportunities in a year, sometimes as few as one. Picking an unqualified prospect can be a tremendous drain of resources.

"Quote and hope" proposals. The client issues a request for proposal (RFP) and a new salesperson thinks, "Great, somebody's going to buy something," so he dashes back to the office and cranks out a huge response.

The salesperson jumps on a white horse and gallops out to the client. But the drawbridge to the castle is up, so he circles around the walls trying to get access. No way. In frustration, he heaves the proposal over the wall hoping it hits someone important. There it lands, *plop*, in the middle of the courtyard. He hopes somebody picks it up and becomes so excited a contract is heaved back over as he waits on the other side.

This is not control selling. These are sales SCUDs—unguided sales missiles. What you need is a laser-guided missile to focus the right issues on the right people rather than lobbing expensive proposals over the wall. *Proposals don't sell, people do.* The win rate of responses to unsolicited proposals is very low. The veteran knows that if you didn't help define the requirements, someone else probably did.

Ineffective team selling. In many cases technical product or service teammates are involved on a sales team. Their number one complaint is that the sales reps keep the strategy to themselves. The rest of the sales team doesn't know the plan, the strategy, or what issues to emphasize to which key buyers in time to prepare.

The result is often a misguided or canned presentation that misses the mark.

Dashing to the demo. The key to consultative selling is to determine clients' needs first. It's even better if you help them determine what their needs are. If you first learn of an opportunity when the requirements definition lands on your desk, you have already missed the first step in the sales cycle. You are, to some degree, already out of control, especially if somebody else wrote the requirements.

In order to link your solutions into the client's business problem you must have an understanding of the industry, culture, competitors, clients, and politics. In product-oriented companies, especially those with product superiority, the product sometimes serves as a crutch, and salespeople get the feeling that, "If we can just show this to them, they'll be overwhelmed."

This approach may work for a while if you have clear product superiority. But in today's high-tech world, product superiority may last only a matter of months, and competitors quickly reach "demo parity." In this approach, all the linking of capabilities to benefits is left up to clients or their consultant. It's almost impossible to give a tailored, focused presentation when you haven't spent time face-to-face with the client before the presentation.

Moreover, a needs analysis can be much more than just a discovery process. The competitive battle is often won in the face-to-face meeting *before* the presentation. The outcome of the majority of sales are pretty well determined *before* the capabilities demo.

Little white lies. Joe Isuzu was a character in an automobile commercial in the United States several years ago who told outrageous, giant lies that couldn't possibly be true. It produced quite a funny commercial. *In reality, the person who gets lied to the most, is often the salesperson.* Or sometimes the information they get ends up not being the truth, which is different, but just as disastrous.

While I was on a sales call to a distillery in Kentucky, the chief financial officer and the chief information officer both made the statement in polite conversation: "I'm not sure where the project stands right now." After leaving the prospect, I said to the salesperson, "This is my first call on this account, but it doesn't smell right. If the top two officers of this company don't know where a project of this magnitude stands, there is no project. Or they may be dodging the question."

We created an opportunity to stop back by that afternoon to drop off some additional information for a project team member, and guess what we found? Those two officers were in a meeting with our competitor negotiating a contract! We were the safety net in case they couldn't come to terms with the competition.

Dead and Don't Know It

Why is it so difficult for salespeople to get an accurate under-standing of where they are in the complex sale? The reason is that it's to the customer's advantage to keep you in the dark. As long as they can do that, they have control. *And if you knew where you really stood in these sales, you might go away, and they don't want that to happen—yet.*

Rarely does a client say to a vendor, "You really don't have a chance of winning this business. You need to try somewhere else." It's to their advantage to keep at least three vendors in the hunt. Why?

1. *Due diligence.* They need to show they studied the leading vendors in the marketplace. In case this project fails, they don't want to be accused of not having made a studied decision.

2. *Price leverage.* After the vendor is selected, the acquisition phase starts, and they will need multiple vendors at that point to drive the price down. This is called "commodification."

3. *Safety net.* If they can't come to legal terms and conditions with their first choice, they will need a backup alternative.

4. *Lack of knowledge.* It's not always an intentional lie. Perhaps they tell you what they think is true, and *they* get fooled. Many of these clients have never been in evaluations where political activity has erupted.

5. *Lack of courage to tell you you're losing.* Maybe they like you personally, but your company or your solution is not winning, and they just can't bear to give you the bad news.

The average competitive salesperson gets a great deal of misinformation or, in some cases, no information. Information is the radar of strategy. Without it, many salespeople are flying blind through a cloud bank.

Because misinformation is such a critical part of the complex sale, anyone who takes one person's opinion on anything will be a perpetual victim. Information must be constantly cross-checked and triangulated by multiple sources to get to the real truth and to find out who consistently has it and who doesn't.

Remember When We Lost That Deal

Who do we go see when we discover our deal is out of control? The sales manager, of course.

You say, "Boss, we've got to talk. I've been meaning to travel with you more, and I've got a good place we can start. Oh, by the way, put on your asbestos gloves, because this account's on fire."

Salespeople used to come into my office and say, "You've got to call this CEO and tell him his people don't understand their own requirements. They're believing all the lies of the competitors. They're using the wrong process, and they're going to make the wrong decision."

"Let's see. I'm supposed to call their CEO, whom I've never met, and basically say, 'Your people are stupid. And since they work for you, you must be stupid, too. So could we have lunch and do business?'" Obviously, this strategy has little chance of success and may scorch the earth in this account forever.

Instead, I'd sit them down and ask a few questions.

● "Did we help generate the requirements?" "*No.*"
● "Was our point of entry high or low?" "*Purchasing agent.*"
● "Did we remember to trap this competitor's weakness with our friends? You know if they present first, they're hard to beat. But a few well-placed questions causes their presentation to come apart." "*No, we didn't do that.*"
● "Did we have a team strategy session before the presentation?" "*There wasn't time.*"
● They haven't delivered what they've sold. "Did we remember to raise the reference issue?" "*No.*"

At this point, I advise salespeople all they can do is what General Custer did when he was completely surrounded, and his chief scout asked, "General Custer, what's our strategy?"

He replied, "First thing we need to do is make a note to ourselves—*never get in this situation again.*"

I would tell salespeople, "You took a bullet a while ago, you just didn't know when to die and fall down."

It is possible, but not probable, to turn this deal around at the last minute. Multimillion-dollar deals have been turned around in the last hour. *But the key is not to get into this position in the first place.* Early prevention beats error correction. There are many things that can be done to gain better control of the complex sale from the very beginning—if we have a process.

We can never really gain "control" of the client's evaluation; there are too many variables, and we have no authority. But better control at each point means we can allocate our resources and time where we have a reasonable chance of winning. "Control" doesn't mean manipulation. It means *understanding* the client's problem better, linking our solution to those problems in a better way, differentiating our solution in a professional manner, and earning trust by outperforming the competition.

A very important part of navigation is knowing when you're lost. The space shuttle is technically off-course ninety-nine percent of the time, but it has a process that identifies exactly when and how much it is off-course and corrects itself thirty-three thousand times a second. Salespeople need a system that tells them, in advance, whether their strategy is winning and how to change their strategy in time if it is not.

There are many forces in today's complex sale to cause a sales effort to go off-course, because there is a sea change in progress in complexity for salespeople as a result of changes in the ways customers buy.

CHAPTER 2

What Makes Today's Complex Sale Complex?

The business revolution is sweeping away many of the traditional ways of working, of interacting with customers. If we don't change, if we don't embrace the future, we will be left behind.

Larry Wilson
Stop Selling, Start Partnering

The successful salesperson of the next twenty years must become a team leader and more—*he or she must be the CEO of a virtual corporation.* In competitive evaluations, the salesperson of the future must lead two to twelve people on a sales team that is selling to twenty people or more on a buying committee. And the sales team will change from account to account.

The role of personality, persuasion, and aggressiveness will always be important to any sales function. However, they are no longer enough. We must not only sell hard; we must also sell even smarter than ever before.

New models of selling demand new skill sets, a better understanding of the client's business, and the ability to work collaboratively to solve business problems rather than to sell products. The challenges of change for today's salesperson are many.

13

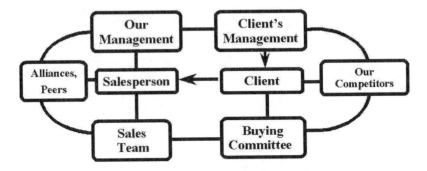

The Marketing Molecule

Figure 2-1 *The diagram depicts the "marketing molecule" of relationships that a salesperson must manage today. Today's salespeople must sell up, down, and laterally, both inside their own organization as well as to the client and outside to third-party partners and distributors. The most effective build a strong personal network of resources within their own firms, as well as the industry, to get things done.*

- *Selling solutions vs. selling products.* Buyers are ready to pay more and give competitive advantage to those companies who provide results rather than tools. Selling solutions means reducing risks by taking responsibility for service, integration, customization, implementation, or whatever other business processes solve the whole problem for the client rather than just a part of the problem.

- *Competitive selling.* Competitive selling isn't negative selling unless it's done wrong. The salesperson in a competitive sale has to walk a fine line between passive and proactive competition. The salesperson who discusses the competition too early or too aggressively will be perceived as unprofessional or defensive. But one who doesn't differentiate or control the issues will be in constant reaction mode. What is appropriate differs by situation, culture, and the relationship with the *individual* buyer. The ethical premise of competitive selling is first, *your solution is genuinely good for the client's organization,* and second, *your tactics remain morally, legally, and ethically sound.* If the former is not true, you should get out of the account. If the latter is not true, you should get out of the business.

- *Long sales cycles.* During a lengthy sales cycle the relative importance of issues will change. New requirements and new players will emerge. So a time-based sales strategy must be used to focus the right issues and tactics on the right people at the right time.

● **Services vs. products.** Selling intangible solutions and services is a different process from selling tangible products—but it shouldn't be, *if a consultative approach is used*. The sales models and terminology are different, but there are different paths to the end result, which is a solution for the buyer.

● **Multiple buyers.** The skills of the business developer and much of the sales training of the past years have been aimed at selling to individuals. This forms a solid foundation. There are techniques for selling to individuals, however, that not only *won't* work in a group environment, but they may actually backfire. Multiple buyers with individual agendas lead to political activity. Failure to anticipate this aspect of business decision making can find salespeople with superior solutions blindsided and outsold.

● **Executives buy differently.** Strategic solutions necessitate the involvement of the client's executives in the sales cycle. Quite often, these solutions have technical foundations that necessitate involvement of technical buyers in the sales cycle as well.

Executives buy different benefits from your solution than technical project team members will. These two groups buy differently and speak different languages. Each group is important to the complex sale. But, it's as if they receive on different frequencies. If you sell to either group on the wrong bandwidth, you will be ineffective.

Account Management and Repetitive Selling

The gateway to repeat business and account management is performance. A short-term oriented, predatory sales force can actually be a long-term sales prevention force. Unless you exceed expectations of most clients and delight a few, you will not build a foundation of customer loyalty. Account management means building company-to-company trust that results in less competitive, more profitable repeat business.

In their book, *The Discipline of Market Leaders*, Michael Treacy and Fred Wiersema refer to "customer intimacy" as one of three value disciplines (along with product leadership and operational excellence). "Customer-intimate companies continually deepen their client's dependence on them. One job well done begets another as the client's confidence grows. The company uses this closeness to increase its understanding of the client's business. The process builds upon itself."[1]

Project vs. Process Account Management

To some account managers "opportunities" mean periodic competitive evaluations, the primary focus of this book. But in certain industries such as pharmaceuticals, consumer package goods, industrial supplies, and commodities, much of account management is not focused on competitive buying events but a flow of products through a channel.

These two sales models are as different as make-to-order manufacturing is to process manufacturing. A consumer package goods account manager for a major retailer, for example, probably doesn't go through committee evaluations of each new product.

What are called opportunities in process- or flow-type account management selling may include the following:

- Joint marketing promotions
- Cooperative advertising
- Introduction of a new product
- Making it easier to buy from us
- Opening new stores or markets
- Supply chain and inventory management
- Quality or problem resolution
- Vendor-managed inventory

The term *customer relationship management* encompasses all aspects of satisfying and retaining existing customers. Often the trusted relationship may be the only advantage, especially where the product is a commodity. But the differences between "project" and "process" account management should not be ignored in selecting team talent, training methodologies, and sales force automation technology. Many firms are using the wrong tools, training, or talent for their sales model.

Team Selling

Technical products, broad product lines, and channel distribution partners mean selling through other people—most or all of whom don't report to the account manager. Keeping the team informed of the strategy and focused on the right issues requires leadership, a common language, and effective communication tools.

Multilevel Sales

There are four levels of direct business-to-business selling—industry marketing, account management, opportunity management, and individual level selling (see Figure 2-2). The foundation of all selling is, of course, *individual selling at the tactical level*, because someone must sit across the desk and persuade someone else. A single buyer and a single seller make up a simple sale, although this doesn't mean it's easy. And for many years this was the only level of awareness in selling.

But in selling systems and solutions that touch multiple departments of an organization, decisions are often made by buying

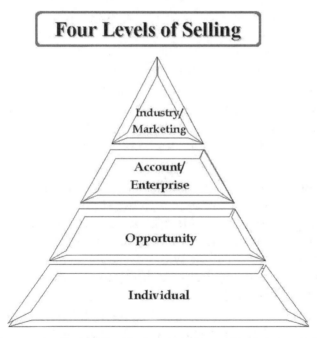

Figure 2-2 *There are four levels of direct business-to-business selling. Industry marketing defines our firm's go-to-market approach to a vertical industry. Our account plan is our strategy to dominate a major enterprise account with a consistent plan worldwide. Opportunities are buying events, often competitive and committee driven. Individual selling is the persuasion of individual stakeholders to recommend you. Each requires different methodologies, talent, and tools but an integrated overall plan. Smaller firms or smaller accounts may not utilize all levels.*

committees in *competitive evaluations* that are referred to as "opportunities." Larger accounts or global enterprises may warrant an additional investment in *account or enterprise management* resources to lead and coordinate sales and service efforts. Many smaller firms are already concentrated in a single industry, but some larger ones must choose to focus on select vertical or *industry markets* with different expertise, strategies, and competitors.

The industries that use this model are *information technology, consulting, medical, telecommunications,* and *financial services,* where the solution affects multiple departments and has perceived strategic value as opposed to a commodity. Most of the larger organizations deploy sales forces by industry segment for their major accounts. This approach enables focused industry solutions and industry-knowledgeable consultative salespeople.

Usually you must penetrate and gain a toehold in an enterprise before you can move to account management. In large accounts, however, opportunity strategy should align with an overall, cohesive account strategy and its goals, if one is to move to account dominance. Consequently, unless you are in a small account, *strategy should be driven at all four levels.*

The next level of strategy from opportunity management is not only *up* to account management, but *down* to the stakeholder level. *After all, companies don't buy; people do.* People decide as individuals before they decide as a committee.

Each of these levels of selling requires different sales models, different talent, and different tools. From a hiring perspective, this means getting the right people into the right jobs. From a training point of view, it may mean developing a curriculum of integrated courses rather than just one. And from a technology view, contact management software alone will not enable a team to share a strategic plan for a major account, so different technology is needed at higher levels of selling.

The difficulty for salespeople in controlling competitive evaluations is that often the client is not in control of the process themselves. Let's take a look in more depth at the perils involved in competitive evaluations and how they can quickly fly off course unless your people are prepared to manage them.

CHAPTER 3

The Canyon and the Crucible—The Competitive Evaluation

Unlike the process of qualification, which is predominately rational, logical, and based on facts, the selection stage is mostly intuitive, personal, and based on impressions.

David Maister
Managing the Professional Service Firm

Competitive selling of big-ticket items usually results in comparative evaluations. Several vendors are invited into the process, quite often with a request for proposal. In the initial screening process, several competitors are evaluated in detail by a committee of buyers from different departments.

Usually there is only one competitor that emerges victorious. There are no silver medals; second place pays zero. Victor or victim—it is an all-or-nothing game.

The Death Valley Sales Cycle

Although these evaluations start out in a logical mode, there is a point where they often turn from a logical and rational information-gathering process to an emotional and political selection process. This happens at the point where the buying committee has to make a decision.

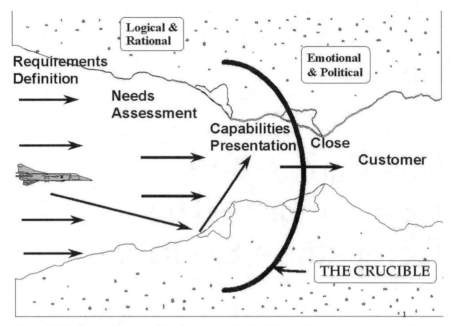

Figure 3-1 *To the vendors, the evaluation process is like flying a plane into a box canyon. You may get in, but it's hard to get out intact. And the further you go in, unless you know the way out, there is no place to turn, and you can't climb out. Unless you win, these evaluations can be the black hole of resources for your organization.*

For years, sales managers have used the analogy of a funnel to describe the flow of leads to prospects to closes. This implies that gravity alone will cause a certain number of opportunities to become clients. However, the canyon metaphor implies that the salesperson, like a pilot, can choose where to navigate, and he or she can influence events to emerge successfully. Likewise, salespeople have sensors (questions) that detect obstacles and let them know where they are at all times so they can correct when they are off-course lest they hit the canyon walls.

At some point the canyon narrows. It is what we call the decision-making *crucible*. In chemistry a crucible is where things heat up—like politics; where things melt down—like the decision-making process; and if a lid is put on it, pressure builds and it often explodes into a power struggle. Likewise, political pressure rises when a client must make a decision where multiple stakeholders have not reached a consensus. We have seen multimillion-dollar deals turn in twenty-four hours during this emotion-packed period.

The client often starts under the illusion that, because of the committee involvement in gathering information and analysis, everyone will reach a happy consensus for a single vendor. This scenario seldom happens.

As the evaluation approaches the crucible, the client typically has some people on the committee who want one vendor for some reasons, other people who want other vendors for other reasons, and some people who want no change at all. But they must make a decision. Or as one of our clients said, "They don't decide how to decide until they can't decide."

In the crucible of a buying evaluation, there are three typical scenarios.

Scenario 1—Issues Shift

In this situation, several vendors have a solution or a product that *could* do the job. At that point, the issues in the evaluation change in importance. Product functionality declines as an issue, and the client turns to nonproduct differentiators such as company strength, price, service, or relationship. A savvy salesperson can use this turbulent time to refocus the issues to their strengths and off of their weaknesses. Or someone less savvy can be blindsided by these changes and be caught selling the wrong things to the wrong people.

Scenario 2—Divided Camps

In this case, nobody has everything the client needs. One vendor has some needed functionality, another has some attractive features, and a third has some things the client likes, but the client can't get it all from one vendor. In this scenario, a power struggle often erupts.

You had better be riding the right horse into this battle, because *at this point the power of your capability is only as good as the political power of the client sponsor who wants it—or the magnitude of the business problem that it solves.* You must have either powerful people or urgent business problems working for you—or plan to lose.

Scenario 3—Loss of Momentum

Our biggest competitor is often "no action." Some companies lose one-third of their forecast pipelines to companies that evaluate and then don't buy anything. The result is a terrible waste of resources.

Opportunities stall because neither business pain nor power sponsors are present to drive the opportunity into a sale. Nobody inside the client organization can sell the proposal internally and deliver a value proposition strong enough to cause anyone to take action. The risks of changing begin to rise; no one can sell the chief financial officer or the decision makers; and the deal comes to a stalemate.

Quite often, salespeople don't recognize what is happening in this situation. Without good information from inside the buying committee, salespeople often cruise along until they get the bad news too late to do anything about it. This is when the deal goes out of control.

The first step to gaining control is to get control of ourselves. We must build our sales team with the right talent in the right jobs for each account.

CHAPTER 4

Talent and Team Selling:
Tellers, Sellers, Hunters, Farmers, Business Developers, Partners, and the Industry-Networked Consultant

> *If you're a middleman, the Internet's promise of cheaper prices and faster service can "disintermediate" you, eliminating your role of assisting the transaction between the producer and the consumer.*
>
> Bill Gates
> *Business @ the Speed of Thought*

Key Questions
- *How do I structure my team-selling sales model?*
- *How do my customers buy?*
- *Do we sell the way that they buy?*
- *What talent and skills do I need to go to market?*
- *Do I have the right people in the right sales roles?*
- *Can I grow to the next level of sales competency?*

Sell the Way the Customer Buys— Use the Right Sales Model
The state of the art of selling didn't change much from the Industrial Revolution to the 1980s, but it has changed dramatically since. Although some of the terms have been used

23

simplistically for years, I have defined seven generations of buyer-seller relationships to describe the evolution of sales talent levels over the last twenty years.

This model describes the potential growth paths and skill sets to the next level of competency for salespeople and the different roles individuals play in the team sale. We call these tellers, sellers, farmers, hunters, business developers, partners, and the industry-networked consultant.

Each role requires different skill sets, different strategies, and different methodologies. Getting the wrong talent in the wrong job or selling one way to a client who buys another way, can be fatal to sales effectiveness. Identifying the skills and traits that predict success in each role and the interviewing questions that accomplish this is a process that has taken years to build.

Seven Generations of Buyer-Seller Relationships

Seller	Buyer
Industry-Networked Consultant	Network
Partner	Partner
Business Developer	Sponsor
Farmer	Repetitive
Hunter	Competitive
Seller	Consultative
Teller	Commodity

Figure 4-1 *The seven generations of selling correspond to seven patterns of client buying behavior. Often a large company will have clients in all types. A sales model that matches talent and technique to the way that the client buys allocates resources where they will have the greatest effectiveness.*

In the early stages of growth, companies frequently need prospecting or hunting salespeople to build share. If the solution is complex or high-tech, technical experts or support people become involved in the sales process. As market share grows, repetitive business to existing clients becomes increasingly important. And as global enterprise clients grow, they may require additional account management resources.

In smaller companies, salespeople often fill multiple roles. Unfortunately, the skill sets for each type of selling are different. The challenge is to get the right people in the right jobs and allocate resources where they will have the greatest return.

The essence of strategy is to allocate resources to the place and time that exploits the competitor's weaknesses. Failure to understand one's sales model and how it is changing can result in an ineffective market strategy and misallocation of sales resources.

Ten Laws of Team Selling

For sales managers, building a model that deploys sales talent in the most productive way is an ongoing challenge. In working with some of the largest sales organizations in the world, we have seen the following best practices emerge in the development and allocation of sales talent:

1. Different levels of selling require different methodologies and different talent.
2. Depending on your size and solution, you may have people in all roles on a sales team. Get the right people in the right jobs.
3. Everyone should grow their skill set from teller to consultative seller. An industry-focused sales force promotes greater knowledge of client issues.
4. There are different development paths to partner level selling: the client path, the consultative path, and the competitive path.
5. Growing from one sales role to another requires new skills and attributes that may be dormant or missing. Not all people are willing or able to grow to the next level.
6. Allocate sales team resources according to how the customer buys. Don't try to partner with commodity buyers.
7. Don't put tellers or farmers into competitive sale situations without a hunter.
8. It is a waste of talent to have hunting salespeople farming noncompetitive, small-order, repeat business.
9. Turnover of account managers (or sponsors) usually clears the registers of relationships built.
10. Make sure everyone working on the account knows the sales strategy and plan.

If we plot these selling styles with client intimacy on one axis and competitive effectiveness on the other, we see multiple career development paths for salespeople.

The Seven Generations of Selling
Building Your Sales Talent Model

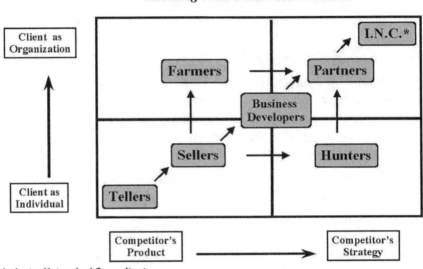

* Industry Networked Consultant

Figure 4-2 *The seven generations of selling correspond to seven ways that buying organizations buy. Each style of selling requires a different skill set, talent level, and methodology. A sales team may have people in each role on an engagement. While everyone should grow from telling to consultative selling, further career growth can either be through the client, business development, or hunter route. Not all partner-level salespeople evolve through competitive selling.*

The Teller

Although product knowledge is important for credibility, tellers feel they can simply explain enough features about the product or service that eventually they will hit something the client likes. Linkage of features to benefits is left to the buyer.

Before computers, tellers showed with slide trays, showing feature after feature: "Stop me if you see something you like." And if the client didn't surrender, they had another slide tray. Today we have presentation software with even greater capacity to bore our prospects.

Early in my sales career as an account manager, I was in the back of the room while one of my product specialists was presenting a system. We were extremely proud of the functionality and about halfway through the presentation, our product rep put up a slide and said, "Now, if you were a hospital, you'd really like this feature."

What!? I was utterly stunned. I thought to myself, "They're *not* a hospital—they're a *bank!* They're *never* going to be a hospital; they'll *always* be a bank!"

How preposterous, the idea of showing a hospital feature to a bank.

But this is no less preposterous than showing somebody a solution to a problem they don't have—or a feature for which they have no need. You might as well show a hospital feature to a bank.

Ready, Fire, Aim

Even with the advances in today's selling, tellers still lapse into endless parades of product features without connecting them to benefits. Presenting features in search of problems is called "shotgun selling," "spray and pray," or in the vernacular of the trade "show up and throw up." In some cases, it's pride in product functionality that causes it. Or sometimes technical salespeople feel that if you just show them how smart you are, they'll buy from you, so you tell 'em everything you know whether they need it or not.

If this is all the value a salesperson can bring (some of them don't even know their products well enough to do this), then this type of salesperson is an endangered species. Because if telling is all you can do, there are cheaper, more effective ways to get this done. Internet, multimedia, channel marketing, or catalog sales will replace this type of selling. And good riddance to it!

Many of the worst examples of unprofessional selling come from the auto industry. Several years ago, a car dealer in St. Petersburg, Florida, fired his entire sales force and sales went up twenty-six percent. *Up twenty-six percent!* This wasn't a sales force—they were actually getting in the way. Why? Because once you decide which kind of car you want to buy, it's now a commodity. It doesn't take a salesperson to sell a commodity.

Most of these people don't even know their own products. Dealing with them is an awful experience, especially in negotiation. This Florida car dealer said, "You're a smart buyer. Here are the keys, test drive it. If you want to buy it, come back and we'll talk about financing. The price is the price. Our prices are lower because we've cut out these thirty-thousand-dollar dead weights." It's a phenomenon known as the "no-dicker sticker." And now Carmax, AutoNation, and other dealerships are doing the same thing. The point is that if you can't bring value as a salesperson, there are cheaper and more effective ways to distribute. The same change has impacted bank tellers and stockbrokers.

Dell Computers effectively used technology to free up salespeople from processing orders to more significant tasks. In his book, *Business @ the Speed of Thought*, Bill Gates describes the reaction of Dell's sales force to the effects of disintermediation: "Dell salespeople had already begun to play a consultant's role, helping the customer develop technology migration plans and leasing and asset replacement programs and understanding the customer's business well enough to recommend ways that technology could help the bottom line more."[2] Of course, this means developing new skills and competencies for the salesperson.

The Consultative Seller

Questions are the answer.

Zig Ziglar, *Ziglar on Selling*

The first step from art to science in selling came from a consultant named Neil Rackham in his book, *Spin Selling*.[3] He had been commissioned by large companies to perform some of the first observations of salespeople to figure out what the successful ones did right and what the unsuccessful ones did wrong.

He came to an interesting conclusion that was not expected: The best salespeople were not necessarily the best talkers. They were the best listeners. Listen first, talk second. This was the birth of consultative selling. Let's find the need first *before* we present a solution.

This approach is quite natural for consultants and quite difficult for product salespeople, especially those with product superiority who are eager to talk about it. Rackham found that the best salespeople had a much higher listen-to-talk ratio. They used the classic tools of probing—who, how, what, why, when, and where—as well as reflexive probes such as, "Oh, tell me more," to keep the client talking.

> Two ears, one mouth—maybe God had something in mind.

This discovery process prevents a multitude of sins. One, it's better for qualification in determining whether you have a fit before you present a solution. You may choose to disqualify the client based on the information gathered. Two, it prevents presumptive selling: "How dare you present a solution? You don't even understand my problem." And three, listening builds rapport between seller and buyer.

Even if the seller knows what the client's problem is—this is called selling to *anticipated* needs—it doesn't matter. Admitting a problem helps buyers open up and share the pain; it makes them more receptive to suggestions and solutions.

In a single sales call, this means probing and listening before we present. In the case of a formal presentation, this means a needs analysis or survey is essential before a presentation. This is quite natural to consultants, where the solution is defined by the problem.

But many product companies have fallen into the trap of dashing to the demo. And when competitors achieve "demo parity," their product superiority is no longer apparent and sales tumble along with your stock price, because salespeople have used product superiority as a crutch and fallen out of the habit of listening first and talking second.

A client company of ours found that its dominant product was suddenly beginning to lose to a new competitor whose system had less functionality. It wasn't a matter of product superiority—it was the way in which it was being sold. The dominant product presenters were so proud of their functionality they spent eight full hours showing endless features.

Their competitor's strategy was "less is more." With less functionality, they emphasized simplicity and ease of use, and they did a better job of listening. They came to the client, rolled up their sleeves, and said, "What do you want this system to do?" Then they listened.

When they presented, they focused like a rifle on the pains the client had confessed. The superior product company marched in with an entourage of people, spent eight hours shotgunning features, and fell into the trap of appearing to be too complex.

In response, the company with the dominant product decided to change its selling strategy. They cut their demos from eight hours to two hours— and they were better! They were more effective because they were always preceded by a two- to four-hour needs analysis a week before the demo. The intent of the needs analysis was to focus the presentation so it didn't appear too complex. But they found a tremendous bonus in the needs assessment, face-to-face phase of the sale. They discovered many things could be influenced in the competitive sales cycle before the presentation that could not be achieved in the demo.

They found building rapport was easier elbow-to-elbow, facing the same direction. They discovered clients were more willing to confess problems and pains. They learned they were able to stimulate dormant demand and raise issues that worked to their advantage on an individual basis, which could not be achieved in front of a group of strangers. They were able to get better competitive data, better information on corporate culture and terminology, and learn the inner secrets of politics in the company.

The effect was dramatic. During presentations they had friends in the audience, they were focused on things that the client wanted to hear, they knew who had the bigger votes, and they knew who was playing which role in the decision. They were able to raise issues that highlighted their strengths or focused on the weaknesses of the competitor—in half the time.

The Hunter

The hunters make things happen. They are the fighter pilots of the sales world. They understand how to defeat the competitor's strategy as well as their product. The hunter focuses on winning competitive, comparative evaluations, quite often in new-name business. They are at their best when they face obstacles and competition. They influence, to the degree they can, the competition, the politics, and the process to their advantage.

Effective hunters understand how to pick the right battles and get the competition to react to them. They have an acute nose for politics. They know how to deal with the client as an organization, not just with the individuals involved.

Moreover, today's salespeople are at the nucleus of a marketing molecule. They must lead a team of two to twelve people to deal with a committee of two to twenty people on the client's side. And since none of these people actually report to them, authority means little; influence and common goals mean everything. *Consequently, selling inside your own company is as important, and often more difficult, as selling outside.*

As leader of a virtual sales team, or several, they need a keen sense of politics and power in an organization, because likewise, their clients are moving from hierarchical organizational structures to cross-functional process and project teams.

The weakness of great hunters, however, is that they are often not focused on repeat business. If a hunter runs down the road to the next hot deal and doesn't stay around and deliver customer satisfaction and results, or tosses it over the wall to the project leader and disappears, they may be doing deal management, but they are certainly not doing account management. This happens too often in publicly-owned companies because of short-term focus from quarterly sales quotas.

Knowledgeware was a company you may not have heard of because they don't exist anymore. They joined the graveyard of companies that didn't understand when their sales model changed from one-and-done selling to repeat-business selling. The company sold computer-aided software engineering when it was a hot new product.

But a technology shift from mainframes to client-server changed the buying model to allow the purchase of initial pilot projects rather than a full enterprise commitment. Their sales-people would secure an order for ten workstations in a departmental pilot and then run on down the road, capturing one after another of these.

The company was proud of their motto, "We sell tools, not solutions." The problem was that nobody stayed with the customer to make sure they knew how to use the product effectively to build applications and solve business problems. Consequently, they built an eighty-percent market share—of unhappy clients.

They inoculated their own marketplace. Their stock fell from forty to four dollars a share, and they vaporized over half a billion dollars' worth of stockholder value before they were acquired.

Companies that have growing market share must eventually make the transition to repetitive selling into the customer base. Repeat business means moving from opportunity management to a process of account management, which requires different strategies and talent. For many consumer package goods, industrial, and medical salespeople, customer relationship management is the entire game.

The Farmer

If your solution is complex enough to require an on-site support person to help the client implement it, and if your solution can generate repeat business, then the best salesperson on the second sale is often the project manager on the first sale. They are the advance scouts for repetitive selling, where greater profitability lies.

The definition of the farmer in sales is changing. In the past, the farmer was responsible for delivering the product or solution, providing customer service, and responding to the customer—a caretaker. This will always be an important function for client satisfaction and references. The farmers' new responsibilities, however, make them an integral part of the sales team. If they think their job is to keep the customer quiet, produce eight billable hours, and go home, they are suffering from an outdated, short-sighted vision of their job.

Their new job is to deliver and document results and, in the process, to make higher and wider contacts in the organization and *to sell between the sales*. They also need to act as listening posts for potential business in the form of dormant needs and latent problems. Their job is to proactively gain the high ground and create preference for their company and their solution *before an evaluation ever happens*.

Although they are not usually competitive salespeople, they should know when to call in the hunters, who are. If you send your farmer up against the competitors' hunter, they'll probably lose.

The Business Developer

Our consulting clients use the title "business developer" not only to avoid the designation of "salesperson," with its many unwanted connotations to consultants, but also because these people *develop* demand rather than *react* to demand. This type of selling has also been called the "prospector" and, in the case of the most successful consulting partners, "rainmaker."

Business developers stimulate dormant or latent business problems into buying action for a solution. They know that if requirements are already defined, the first step is over and a competitive evaluation is coming.

The first step is to find a latent business problem and create a vision of what life could be like if they solve it. They also create a vision of what bad things could happen if it is not solved because their biggest competitor is "no action." This creates a gap between where the client is and where they could be.

The next step is to quantify the gap to define the financial return on investment. Then they must find a sponsor with enough power to whom this gap is politically painful and emotional because, again, *pain doesn't actually come from the problem, it comes from the political embarrassment or the chance for glory*. No pain, no change.

Demand Creation
Gap Analysis

Financial Return

Emotional

Political Gain/Loss

Vision if they do   ## Vision if they don't

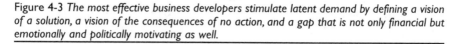

Figure 4-3 *The most effective business developers stimulate latent demand by defining a vision of a solution, a vision of the consequences of no action, and a gap that is not only financial but emotionally and politically motivating as well.*

Demand creation selling sounds hard, and it is. But insurance salespeople do it all the time. No one ever calls and says, "Please, come sell me some life insurance," but billions of dollars of coverage is sold every year. They turn a vision of widows and children in rags and tatters into a vision of retirement and college paid for and then create an emotional call to action.

The Partner

Business partnering was born out of the Total Quality Management movement led by W. Edwards Deming. According to Deming, business partnering to the clients means narrowing the list of vendors to a select few and building preferred or partnering relationships with those. In accounts that practice this model of buying, this means you are either on the inside or the outside. If you're to become an insider, clients are looking for much more from their salespeople than they have in the past. Consequently, for the individual salesperson or consultant, personal growth is not an option.

This term "partnering" has become one of the most misused words in the lexicon of business today. To many buyers it means discounts, and to many vendors it means higher revenues. Partnership is not just repetitive selling at high volumes and discounts.

Done well, it is a powerful process that can transform the adversarial buyer-seller relationship to one of collaboration and then to co-managing the client's business as a trusted advisor.

The essence of partnering is trust: trust in the company, trust in the product or service, and trust in the individual. It comes from a confidence, borne of experience, that over the long term neither party will do something at the other's expense. Contracts are necessary to provide a worst-case safety net and a clear understanding of expectations, but the spirit of a partnership exists above and beyond a contract.

To become a business partner, however, you also have to solve higher-level business problems for your clients. You need to understand that your clients have clients of their own. They also have shareholders, the public, the press, competitors, and the government, all of which put tremendous pressure on today's executives. This gets passed down to department heads and project leaders and passed out to the salesperson in the form of sales opportunities.

If you respond simply to the client's request and don't understand what business problem you are being asked to solve, then at best, if you get the business, you are going to get it in a commodity fashion. If you understand the higher-level business problem, however, you can help your client co-manage their business, and you can move up the value chain from commodity vendor to preferred vendor to strategic partner, building trust with your client and advantage over your competitors.

A consultative salesperson must look beyond the customer's needs to the customer's customer. It means collaborating on product design, joint marketing, supply chain and efficiency, problem escalation, and quality. If preferred vendor status is to be achieved, company-to-company trust must be built over the long term. It means linking agendas and staying in the win-win position.

Not every prospect out there is a candidate for a partnering relationship. It is a function of corporate values and culture. There are some companies whose culture simply will not allow them to partner. Until they change at the top, they will always have an adversarial relationship with vendors. If they do not partner with anyone else, this is a sign they will not partner with you.

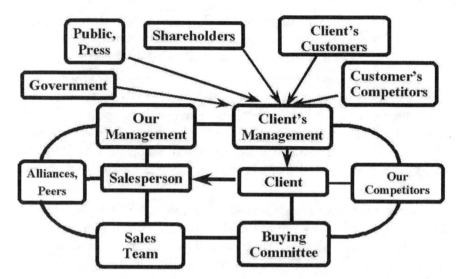

Figure 4-4 *To move from commodity vendor to preferred or partner status, you must link to and solve higher-level problems for your clients. Outside pressures on management result in buying activity by project teams. By tracing a purchasing requirement back to its strategic problem source, you can either validate or disconnect its importance. And by solving the bigger problem, you can command better value and better margins as well as gain access to executives who can shorten sales cycles.*

If you cannot see a way that they will buy on trust (even when you earn it), shorten sale cycles, reduce competition, or increase volumes or margins, then invest your love in another account. There are some clients out there who will drain all your resources and still put you out for bid. An account can be a large account without being a partnership. If you pick the wrong prospects to partner with, you will partner yourself broke.

Larry Wilson has written some excellent books on selling, including *Stop Selling, Start Partnering*. It is a catchy title, but if followed would get you fired in many companies because there aren't enough prospects that buy on the partnering model to make your growth numbers.

Partnerships are built for the long term. In the real world, while building for the long term, you must also make your quarterly numbers or you won't be around to harvest your corn. Unless you are a firm like Andersen or Deloitte, whose strategy is to focus on just those types of clients, you actually need to sell to most accounts *and* partner with those firms that will.

Consequently, unless you are a dedicated large account manager with just one or a few accounts, you must choose a couple of accounts in your territory to invest in this type of relationship while you make your short-term number with the rest. But if you start your year with a couple of "annuity accounts," you can have a head start on achieving your goals.

Moving to this type of selling model will create the need to change—for both salesperson and vendor. Some sales forces talk partnership but do not reward or recognize the behaviors that lead to it. For salespeople this means reengineering your career to bring greater value to your clients by developing industry expertise, strategic literacy, and executive presence.

Industry-Networked Consultant

This type of sales professional has executive and operational contacts built over the years throughout an industry and is seen as an advisor and resource by executives. These salespeople are recognized for *what* and *whom* they know.

One of our principals, John Hille, says this type of salesperson develops his or her own personal "brand" loyalty. Industry-networked consultants speak at industry conferences and are quoted in trade magazines. They help executives find partners, vendors, personnel, and financing. Needless to say, because of their top-down approach, they are not engaged in many competitive evaluations.

They can even become focused on a single account. A former student in one of our classes, when asked what his job was, responded, "My career is selling to Southwestern Bell. I happen to work for a vendor, but I will always sell *to* Southwestern Bell. I worked there, the people trust me, and I know how they work. I may sell for someone else someday, but this will always be my account." It is an interesting and inverted way to define a sales career defined by a single client. But many consulting, banking, and defense industry executives find themselves working within this same model.

Total Sales Force Effectiveness

Successful selling in the complex sales environment in the twenty-first century will take a combination of several elements:

- Technique
- Talent
- Teamwork
- Technology

Technique. Earlier we identified four levels of selling in the complex sale. The methodologies and training are different at each level. Face-to-face training is skills-based and the foundation, since all sales strategies at the tactical level involve persuading someone. Opportunity and account management methodologies must be complete, concise, and integrated. They must be concise enough that they will actually be used by the sales force with a minimum of writing, yet complete enough to provide a winning plan. They must include consultative, competitive, political, and team-selling dimensions in order to win. *The second best sales process finishes second.*

Talent. The seven different talent levels we have identified correspond to seven buying styles of the clients. These models not only provide a career path of personal growth for salespeople, but each selling role is important to the complex sale effort. A sales team may have people in each role assigned to an account. For management, the answer is to profile the skills and knowledge for each job, hire to that profile, and have training processes to help people grow from one level to the next.

Teamwork. The day of the gunslinger is over. Account managers can no longer keep the sales strategy in their heads if they are to lead a team consistently. In order for management to effectively allocate resources, a consistent process that addresses all phases of the sales cycle must be used throughout an organization. In addition, compensation, territory design, reward systems, and revenue split policies should encourage collaboration—*or you will find that often your biggest competitor is yourself.*

Technology. Technology for communicating the sales strategy to the rest of the team is imperative if each of the players is to understand his or her role and if management is to understand the status of each opportunity in the forecast. Sales force automation

(SFA) is currently a booming business because sales is the latest frontier of computerization. Initially most of the focus was on customer relationship management (CRM)—lead tracking, customer information management, order entry, and help desk applications.

A System Is Not A Strategy, Either

But new-name business must usually be penetrated in a competitive situation before we can move to repetitive selling. And the failure rate of SFA among field salespeople is currently high. The reason is that a repository of data without a sales process to turn it into effective differentiation will not yield competitive advantage in an evaluation. *Automated contacts and forecasts, without effective competitive sales plans beneath them will only enable the adding of bad numbers faster.* As these tools address competition, strategy, and politics, as well as benefit maps to individual buyers, the competitive sales rep will start to realize the full potential of these systems.

Once we have our team in place, we need to know what potential advantages we have in our company's arsenal that we can call upon to win.

Individual Development Plan

Personal Value Chain

What objectives do you have to develop or maintain yourself as an industry or management expert? What reading or education plans do you have for the coming year?

Does your client see you as a trusted advisor for issues outside your product or service? What are your plans to move yourself up their value chain? How do you plan to influence their mind share?

To what professional associations do you now belong? What plans do you have in this area in the coming year (speeches, articles, attendance, committees)?

Have you been published in a magazine or trade periodical? Is this a part of your plan?

Political Navigation

Who do you need to meet in the next year in your account/company/industry, and how do you plan to gain access? What objective do you have for that relationship?

Do you keep a database of your network? Do you proactively keep contact?

Performance

What activities do you plan to increase client satisfaction in your account?

Strategic Pain

What ongoing research do you plan to keep up with executive and industry issues in your account?

Teamwork

What plans do you have to develop your personal network inside your own company?

Relationships

What social activities do you plan with your client? To what social activities have they invited you? What other relationship building activities do you plan?

Figure 4-5 *The buyer's rising expectations of consultative salespeople and the impact of the Internet make continuous personal growth an imperative. This plan may be useful in defining a vision and setting goals for career reengineering to the next level of sales competency.*

CHAPTER 5

The Arsenal of Competitive Advantage

Different customers buy different kinds of value.

Michael Treacy, Fred Wiersema
The Discipline of Market Leaders

Key Questions

- ■ *What capabilities and differentiators are we counting on to win?*
- ■ *How does that link to the clients' issues?*

Michael Porter of Harvard says that competitive advantage falls into three categories: You are either the low-price vendor, value differentiated, or focused on a niche market.[4] In differentiating complex solutions, we have identified six major component sources of competitive advantage, each of which has several elements. We call this "the arsenal of competitive advantage." They are potential tools for you to differentiate or create value, but only if you link them to your individual prospect's need.

Value Linkage

Although it is important to be knowledgeable about your company, your offering, and your technology, telling isn't selling. Telling alone leaves the connection of features to benefits up to the client, or someone else like the competition.

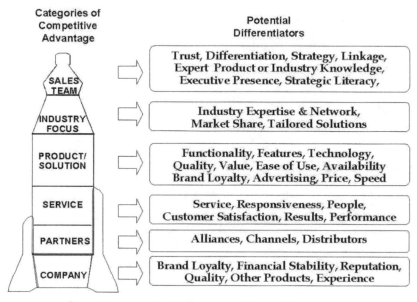

Our Arsenal of Competitive Advantage

Figure 5-1 *Because each individual buyer will buy from a company for a different combination of reasons, it is important that a salesperson understand the arsenal of potential differentiators from which they can draw. The richness of this arsenal is determined by the marketing strategy, innovation, and investment of the firm.*

The task of the consultative salesperson is to take the competitive advantages from the company, the product, and the solution and *focus* it on the business problems of the client. In addition, *value and competitive advantages must be linked to the personal agendas of the right people*, because not all individuals have the same impact on the buying decision, nor do they buy from you for the same reasons. Different advantages must be emphasized at different times to different people, the solution must be differentiated from the competition, and the opportunity must be closed. This means that today's business developer must have a greater understanding of their client's business and industry than ever before.

The process of connecting our advantages to their business problems is called *linkage*. It drives both competitive advantage and value. Linkage of benefits into personal agendas drives individual preference. In today's complex sale, because of multiple buyers and complex solutions, this fundamental sales skill of tying features to benefits has now become a many-to-many challenge. Of the hundreds of potential benefits you could offer, each individual on the buying committee is interested in only a few that matter most to them—but *which* ones?

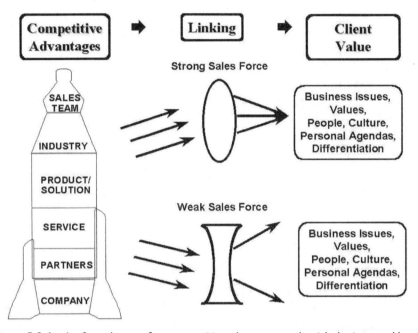

Figure 5-2 *A sales force that can focus competitive advantages on the right business problems, the right people, and the right values at the right time can magnify and focus a company's advantage like a lens. The astute salesperson must know by individual what advantages to link to whom.*

A strong light through a strong lens can burn holes through steel because it is focused. Because they don't understand the client's business or can't connect a solution to the problem, a weak sales force, however, is like a concave lens—it disperses value to the client's eye rather than focusing. It's like looking through a telescope backwards. Clients don't understand why they should buy from this vendor or this company. And quite often they don't.

This ability to perform linkage of solutions to business problems is so powerful that often it means *you don't always need product superiority to win* (although a sales force *does* need a playable

Today's salesperson must have a greater understanding of his or her client's business than ever before.

hand). You simply need one capability connected to one powerful person at the right time in order to win. This is how you can out-sell or be outsold.

> A sale to a high-tech firm in Raleigh, North Carolina, was lost at the last hour. We were leading with nine out of ten people on the committee for nine out of ten weeks. The competitor's salesperson, however, identified one key issue for one powerful person, and she got to him first. She was able to link a capability into that hot strategic issue for this vice president, who in turn was able to convince the entire committee to recommend that vendor. The ultimate irony lies in the fact that we had the capability. Where we lost was our inability to identify the bigger issue, the powerful person, and link our solution. We were outsold.

Because of the complexity of these solutions, proactive linkage is such a key capability to selling in the complex sale, that if you don't do it, the competition may. If a vendor can't do it, clients bring in outside consultants to perform this function. And if no one does it at all, then a terrible thing in selling happens: *nothing*.

If nobody performs this value linkage, then the cost justification or the value proposition fails, concern for risk involved in the project rises, no one can sell it inside to the chief financial officer, the deal stalls and nothing happens. This is as bad as a loss because the same resources were expended and the client bought nothing from anyone.

Done well, however, linkage to strategic issues creates not only competitive advantage but also higher value and usually a larger, more profitable deal. Thus it is often easier to win a large deal than a small one—if you sell the right issues to the right people.

> For many years, the largest sale in the software industry was the thirty-million-dollar sale of Oracle database software to Boeing Aircraft. The Oracle account executive was Jeff Simpson. When we asked him how he was able to win such a big sale, he shared the following story.
>
> Boeing Aircraft was then in the process of beginning a big new strategic project: the 777 aircraft. Boeing's objective was to

defeat its competitor, Airbus, who was subsidized by foreign governments. This was a major undertaking that meant betting the company for the next twenty years.

At the same time, there was a major culture change taking place in that Boeing recognized it could not build the new aircraft the old way. The old way involved two-dimensional design systems residing on different machines that could not detect conflicts and interferences until all the parts of the aircraft were brought together, at which point a great deal of reengineering took place to make the pieces fit together. The result was not only delay and expense, but lower quality as well.

Moving to three-dimensional, computer-aided design techniques meant that interferences could be detected early and tolerances could be reduced so the parts fit the first time they were brought together. The result would be a major saving in time and money. In addition, there was a strategic benefit to Oracle's customer's customer. If airplanes could be made to a high enough quality standard, then an exception might be made to the FAA rule that two-engine, two-pilot aircraft must be flown over land for two years before they could be flown overseas. If the planes were made to a high enough quality, the FAA exception might be gained, thereby saving Boeing's customer millions of dollars by putting their expensive airplanes into overseas production earlier. This is a double linkage to the customer's customer, the airlines.

Simpson said, "We were not the strategic design team for the 777. However, we were an enabling technology that was uniquely qualified—because of our scalability of the database system—to build a new aircraft a new way, significantly reduce costs, and gain advantages for Boeing's customers.

"Once we built that value linkage, thirty million dollars was no longer a large number. That's a rounding error to Boeing. This is one part of one aircraft, and they're going to build thousands of them over the next few years. In addition, we became an integral part of the team and gained a measure of insider status."

At a marketing strategy level, some companies rely on different sources of competitive advantage at different times. For example, IBM relied on company strength and service for many years while it was dominating the mainframe computer business. IBM rarely had the best products the soonest. But it didn't matter. They put the "big blue" label on it (As the saying went, "nobody ever got fired by recommending IBM.") and drowned the client in enough service engineers to provide a technical solution. Clients paid a premium for lower political risk. IBM may not have had the best product at that time, but they certainly had the best solution.

DEC, which at the time had a measure of product superiority through better scalability and portability, never fully capitalized on its advantage because it underestimated the impact of a direct sales team. Management's attitude was that salespeople were a necessary evil and paid them salary with no commission—and not enough of that. Consequently, DEC was never able to fully capitalize its advantage through a hunting sales force.

Ready, Aim, Fire

The role of marketing and product design is to give a sales force as large an arsenal of advantages and benefits as possible. Good hunters don't always need product superiority but they can't hunt with an empty quiver.

The role of the sales force is to link those differentiated capabilities into the personal and professional pains of each buyer individually.

One of the effects of product commodification is a shrinking window of competitive advantage for new products and an increasing lag time for marketing to get the competitive sales message to the field. By the time a sales force figures out how to sell a new product, often the competitor has already reacted. The answer is a fast, replicable process for delivering benefits maps, value propositions, product information, and differentiators to the field. If a salesperson knows he or she will be calling the following day on the chief financial officer of a hospital against a certain competitor, the latest information should be as close as the Web and as fresh as today.

With our team organized and our marketing message of differentiators and advantages in hand, the next thing we need to approach the market is a sales process: R.A.D.A.R.®, our breakthrough process for simplifying the complex sale.

The Solution— R.A.D.A.R.®

CHAPTER 6

R.A.D.A.R.— Simplifying the Complex Sale

Life can only be understood backwards; but it must be lived forwards.

Soren Kierkegaard

We didn't invent the complex sale; the buyers did. Our goal is to simplify it. By combining the intuitive best practices of many of the most effective managers of the complex sale, I have developed a simplified, six-step process that combines consultative, competitive, and political sales principles into a concise yet comprehensive process.

This process was developed by asking dozens of successful sales managers and partners what questions they asked of themselves, their people, and their clients to develop an effective sales strategy. We organized the hundred or so questions into six steps, each of which includes a dozen or more drill-down questions.

Radar has been a major element of victory because *early information* allowed the smaller force to *focus* on the right time and place to meet the enemy. The same principles apply to managing a portfolio of sales opportunities. Our acronym for the R.A.D.A.R. sales process stands for R.eading A.ccounts and D.eploying A.propriate R.esources.™

Concentration of force is the first principle of strategy. Spreading yourself too thin means not concentrating resources on the sales you could win because you are spending time on lower quality prospects. Doing ninety percent of what it takes to win doesn't result in ninety percent of the revenue—it results in zero. You must pick the battles you can win, then win the battles you pick.

Salespeople are busy but they don't get *paid* to be busy. They get paid to win. A planning process for them must be *complete* enough to lead the team but *concise* enough not to slow them down.

The R.A.D.A.R. process has six keys to winning a complex sales opportunity:

Challenges	R.A.D.A.R. Process
Value	**1.** Link Solutions to **Pain (or Gain)**
Resource Allocation	**2.** Qualify the **Prospect**
Competition	**3.** Build Competitive **Preference**
Strategy	**4.** Determine the Decision-Making **Process**
Politics	**5.** Sell to **Power**
Teamwork	**6.** Communicate the Strategic **Plan**

Five of the steps are inputs and the sixth is the plan. Although we will study these steps sequentially, effective salespeople actually perform them simultaneously.

The first step is to learn about the clients' *pains* (or opportunities to *gain)* with a needs assessment. With this information, we will learn enough to *qualify the prospect* for further investment as well as link our solution message to their business problems. As early as the needs assessment (assuming this is not an existing account), we begin to build *competitive preference* for our company, our solution, and ourselves with everyone we meet.

The more we know about the committee's *decision-making process*, the more effective our strategy will be; the more people with *power* involved who prefer us, the better our chances. The better our teammates understand our *plan to win*, the more accurate it will be and the more empowered they will be to leverage their efforts effectively.

The benefits for taking time to communicate a sales strategy include:

- Increases competitive advantage from consistent, effective execution.
- Crystallizes your thinking and forces a decision.
- Provides early detection of blind spots and visibility into the future.
- Leads and empowers your team with a clear direction.
- Prioritizes the urgent from the important.
- Increases your ability to control and manage multiple accounts.
- Develops respect with peers and management.

Competitive advantage will not come from awareness of this process alone but from the consistent *discipline* you apply as a *habit* throughout the sales organization. A manager and mentor of mine, Don House, taught me that "successful organizations make habits of things others don't like to do, or don't find time to do."

In Stephen Covey's book, *The Seven Habits of Highly Effective People,* the fourth habit is "Seek First to Understand." In his model, it is actually the first habit of interdependence with others.[5] It is the basis of the first step of our model—understanding the clients' needs or pains.

CHAPTER 7

Key 1—Link Solutions to *Pain* (or *Gain*)

The new game is based on the ability to help solve significant business problems for the customers. If you want to play, competitive advantage lies in helping your customers make money, save money, or add value to their organization. Understanding your customer's business strategy, market forces, and financial situation is the new core competency.

Larry Wilson
Stop Selling, Start Partnering

Key Questions

■ *Will the pain or opportunity cause them to buy at all? (Urgency)*

■ *Can we solve their problem profitably? (Linkage)*

■ *Can we solve it better than the competition? (Differentiation)*

■ *Can we provide strategic benefits? (Value)*

■ *Are requirements defined? By whom? (Politics)*

Understanding the client's need is the heart of consultative selling. It changes the initial direction of information flow to problems in search of solutions, instead of the other way around.

What problem is the customer trying to solve? Although we use the term "pain," this could also be an opportunity. The art of consultative selling is to get the customer talking in a one-on-one environment, sharing who they are and what they want. Consultative salespeople learn early that the way to get the client talking is to use questions that begin with "who, what, why, where, or when."

This is a critical part of the sale when we begin listening and outcaring the competition, thus building the bonds of rapport that will eventually lead to trust. Even if we know what the pains are, it's not enough. The client needs to *confess* them. Confession is the beginning of behavior modification, and, for a consultant, starts a sharing process that begins to build the bonds of trust. Then, when we do present, we can focus on the needs that have been expressed, in the client's terminology, with friends in the audience, without being set up by the competition.

Understanding the client's need is not always the same as understanding their requirements. Product salespeople too often wait until requirements are defined and the request for proposal lands on their desks. If the requirements have already been defined, you've missed the first step in the sales cycle. But it happens and it's part of the real world. The question is, how were the requirements defined and by whom?

Experience has shown that this is a rather unscientific process on the part of the buyers. They have probably never bought a solution or product of this type, and there are several ways they can proceed to define their own requirements. They can send out a memo to all the end users, saying, "What would you like in this system or solution or product?" They can bring in a consultant. Eventually all the requirements are gathered and sorted into A's, B's, and C's of things they must have and things they'd like to have.

> If the requirements have already been defined, you've missed the first step in the sales cycle.

The key question at this point is, *"In whose opinion?"* Every requirement either has a political sponsor or it doesn't. Every requirement is either connected to a business problem or it's not. Not all sponsors have equal power and not all business requirements have equal impact. Yet these are all thrown into the hopper and pushed out the door in the form of what is commonly known as a request for proposal (RFP), or tender. In some ways it's like the way grandmother made sausage—throw in all the parts, grind it up, and package it. There's an old saying that you really don't want to be around to see sausage being made. But in this case, you need to know exactly how the requirements were made and where each element came from.

> Every requirement either has a political sponsor or it doesn't. Every requirement is either connected to a business problem or it's not. Not all sponsors have equal power and not all business requirements have equal impact.

In the way that requirements are defined lie the seeds of discontent that will burst into a power struggle when clients can't get everything they want from one vendor. You can't assume that a committee made up of multiple buyers really speaks with one voice. The best business developers trace the connections of the requirements back to the sponsors and the business problem. Then they can either link or disconnect those requirements as it suits their strategy.

An electrical utility in Florida sent us a request for proposal (RFP) for a human resource system. In the requirements was a specification that it be delivered under a certain database. We didn't support that database and were not going to. But since they were already a client, it was at least worth a visit to meet with them and qualify the account.

We had access to the chief financial officer and the chief information officer. We said, "We'd like to have your business except for this requirement to operate under a database, one that we don't have. Do you mind if we ask why this database is a requirement?"

The CIO replied, "It's our standard."

"Really? Are all your systems operating under this database?"

"Not exactly," was the reply.

"Then, what percentage of your systems are currently operating under this database?"

"Well," said the CIO sheepishly, "none."

"Let me understand—there are *no* systems operating under this database but it's your standard? Who put this requirement in?"

The CIO admitted that "it must have been one of my people." With the help of a third-party consultant, we found out that the database administrator had planted that requirement. The reason was that he had recommended his company buy that database system two years earlier for about half a million dollars under the promise that systems would be ported over within two years and applications like this could be built in as little as six months. After two years, with considerable expenditure on training and travel, no systems had been built or moved. It was a personal agenda item that was not necessarily good for the company agenda. Once it was exposed as such, the requirement melted away and became a "like to have" rather than a "must have."

But we didn't stop there. We kept peeling back the onion to reveal the real business problem. We asked, "Why have you budgeted money for a new human resource system in the first place?"

The business problem at that time was that they were in a very competitive market for talent in the utilities industry in Florida. If you know that area, you know each city has its own electrical utility—Disney World even has its own. They all compete for talent. This client couldn't attract people to complete mission-critical projects.

We said, "What you need is a human resource system with things like applicant tracking, skills inventory, career development, and flexible benefits so you can attract and retain good people. And it looks like you need it fast. We've successfully implemented a previous system for you, and implemented a system like this in two other cities in Florida in as little as six months. Staffing mission-critical projects is the strategic benefit, and our advantage is speed of implementation."

What happened here? What was the strategy? A greater understanding of the requirements and how they were developed allowed us to (1) disconnect a requirement that we couldn't meet from the real business problem, (2) refocus the buyer on the strategic business problem, and (3) establish linkage between our capabilities and that bigger problem. Actually, the first step was to gain access to executives above the project team, which we were able to get by virtue of our performance in previous engagements. Better information, better strategy, and a turnaround victory.

Dormant vs. Active Pain

Nobody asked for the VCR. Nobody put out a request for Windows software. But customers knew they wanted it when they saw it. These were dormant pains. Neil Rackham showed us that we can sell to expressed or latent pains.[6]

Active pains are those business problems that have been acknowledged by the client and for which they are actively seeking a solution. This is indicated by money being budgeted, project teams being formed, requirements being defined, or vendors being contacted.

The best business developers can find dormant business problems, stimulate them to active pain, and thereby gain an advantage over the competition and perhaps an exclusive opportunity.

In return for finding and stimulating the need, the salesperson needs to gain early advantage, perhaps even an exclusive evaluation. By building preference early, shaping the issues, developing inside sources of information (to the legal extent), and influencing steps in the process, the business developer can accomplish a great deal before the evaluation, even if it must go out for bid.

Personal Agendas and Professional Agendas

One's professional agenda is made up of those goals that are a part of one's job. It is your part of the organizational agenda. Personal agendas are individual goals; sometimes they are aligned with the organizational agenda, and sometimes they are not. When both agendas are met, this has been defined as a "win-win." Those areas of personal agenda that are not aligned with the organizational agenda may or may not represent a conflict of interest.

Personal agenda items are quite often hidden and emotional and cannot be discussed in a group. But they are nonetheless very powerful buying motives, and they must be uncovered. This is one reason we entertain clients outside the office. This is also why establishing rapport and early trust is important.

The speed with which someone will share his or her personal agenda is a function of how quickly you can build trust. This is why the one-on-one phase of selling is so critical. In different countries and cultures, it may take longer to get someone to share his or her personal agenda. In some countries, you must break bread for hours before even discussing business for fifteen minutes. In other countries or parts of countries, you need to establish your competence before you can begin building a relationship. *But each person is an individual and that must be the base level of your strategy.*

Personal agendas and pains are very powerful and not all of them are equal. Maslow and Herzberg[7] showed us that personal needs form a hierarchy. At the base are lower-level satisfiers of safety and survival, and moving up the chain are social needs, and needs for self-esteem and self-actualization. Herzberg called the lower of these satisfiers and the upper of these motivators.

Maslow described it as the "hierarchy of needs." And depending on where we are in life economically and chronologically, different needs take on different priorities at different times. Examples of personal agenda benefits include recognition, promotion, innovation, technical elegance, conformity, retirement, control, money, peer respect, or quality.

As not all personal pains are equal; not all business pains are equal. There is also a hierarchy of business pains, and the powerful ones override the lesser ones.

So What?—Linking Benefits to Pains (or Gains)

Early in a sales career, you learn to connect a feature or capability with a benefit. The feature is what you can do or what the product can do; the benefit is what it could do *for me.* People don't buy drills because they want drills; they buy them because they want holes.

People with technical backgrounds who are new to sales tend to present in terms of features, and early in their sales careers they must learn to connect those to benefits. Two words will help them do that on a consistent basis, because they are the words the clients are asking themselves as you are talking. Those few words are, "*So what?*"

"We have over one thousand employees."

"So what?" the client thinks.

"We have offices in forty cities."

"So what?"

"We have this technical capability."

"So what?" say the clients to themselves.

The simple "so what" test should be recycling inside a salesperson's head whenever he or she is talking to a prospect. When salespeople don't provide the answer to that question, the linkage between your offering and the client's need is left up to the client—or even worse, to the competitor or to some outside consultant—or perhaps it doesn't happen at all. In any event, lack of linking means loss of control and value.

In simple sales this linkage is obvious enough that the customer can do it themselves. These products can be sold over the Internet. But with complex or intangible solutions and multiple buyers, the seller who can best help the client make the connections, face to face and early in the cycle, will usually prevail.

Strategic Pains vs. Tactical Pains

Not all pains or benefits are equal. In selling at the next level—to executives—we need to link capabilities up to the higher-level strategic benefits that executives seek. Get on the right wavelength of the buyer. Sell strategic benefits to strategic buyers and technical benefits to tactical buyers.

One of our clients was finishing a presentation on process manufacturing systems to a client. The graph of the return on investment models for their cost improvements at those volumes looked like a hockey stick as they curved upward after three years. They had done this for a number of major consumer

Food Chain of Value
"The Shark Chart"

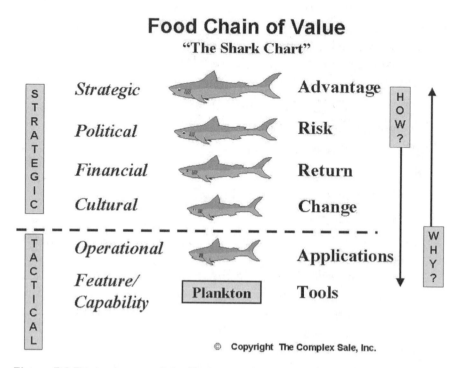

© Copyright The Complex Sale, Inc.

Figure 7-1 *This is what we call the "food chain of values," or our well-known "shark chart," named for the phenomenon that bigger issues tend to eat up smaller ones. Examples of each type follow in this chapter. Executive-level benefits, the ones above the dotted "power line," usually override operational level issues—if the power sponsors are involved. Searching upward for the strategic pain gives reasons for "why" the client needs your operational capabilities. Executives search down for capabilities and tools to answer "how" they will achieve strategic objectives.*

package goods companies and were able to prove the value proposition to the point where the CEO had bought in.

But at the end of the meeting, the CIO, who was the chief technologist, stood up and smirked, "But, sir, you don't understand. This is a nonstandard language and operating system. It's proprietary."

To which the CEO stood up, leaned forward, and said, "I don't care. If they can save us this much money, we don't have to close factories. If they can save us this much money, we don't have to move to Singapore. If they can save us this much money, I can afford another language, I can afford another operating system, I can afford *another IT department!*"

For the money they could save, they could justify *two* IT departments. This was how departmental computing was born and how Digital edged into IBM shops for many years. In the food chain of value, the strategic fish gobbles up the tactical fish just as the strategic benefit devours the tactical benefit—if the right people hear the value proposition.

Operational Benefits

If the decision-making process to select a vendor and to buy now is at the operational level, then operational benefits may be all you need to win an order. Solutions that don't affect multiple departments or strategic issues are often bought at this level, although at commodity prices, since linkage has not been made to higher value benefits. However, this type of sale can be flanked by a competitor with an expanded scope of solution that introduces political, interdepartmental, or strategic issues.

Operational needs are important to the people who actually do the work. They include ease-of-use, efficiency, technical purity, throughput, integration, and functionality. Because tactical buyers often don't see the big picture, sometimes their requirements solve relatively small business problems, or aren't connected to any business problem at all. And if operational needs are at odds with strategic needs (and their sponsors) because they are not available from the same vendor, you can guess which will prevail.

Cultural Benefits

"We weren't selling what they were buying," said Steve Andersen, my district manager explaining why we had lost a sale (he didn't lose many).

"That sounds backwards," I said. "You mean they weren't *buying* what we were *selling?*"

"No, it wasn't a matter of credibility. We didn't sell to the right values of the organization. We misread the culture."

Cultural benefits are extremely important to chief executives who are trying to change or maintain the value systems of their organizations. Companies have personalities, which are defined at the very top. Values and culture are important to executives because that is how they guide employees to do the right things independently when managers aren't there.

To illustrate the importance of these cultural issues, executives who were on pedestals only a few years ago lost their jobs partly because they were unable or unwilling to change culture—Akers at IBM, Stempel at General Motors, Jobs and Scully at Apple, and Olson at DEC. Establishing cultures is not easy, especially when it means aligning personal values of thousands of people with that of the organization. Examples of cultural benefits include empowerment, employee morale, teamwork, flexibility, innovation, global awareness, competitiveness, risk taking, accountability, and quality, to name a few.

In some organizations there is a very cohesive culture throughout, such as in Coca-Cola, Shell Oil, and Federal Express. Some organizations, however, have very divisive and fractional cultures. Each business unit has a separate personality and, quite often, not only do they not get along, but there is also infighting.

One of our clients said this about a large defense contractor with multiple subsidiaries: "Having business at one business unit not only doesn't help me at the next one, it can actually hurt me. They hate each other so much that if one business unit is for me, the other ones will be against me. But they are all united in one value: They hate corporate. So the potential for working my way to the corporate offices and coming down as their worldwide standard is impossible in an account like this. Our best strategy is to pick these business units off one at a time because navigation and influence between them are very limited."

Culture starts at the top. If you can demonstrate how your solution can help a chief officer enable culture change, you can get their attention. Two of our largest pieces of business came from chief operating officers who wanted culture change. One was a product company that wanted to become more consultative, and one was a consulting company that wanted to become more competitive while still staying on the high ethical plane.

Financial Benefits

Financial benefits include return on investment, cost reductions, revenue gains, productivity, cash flow, reduced inventories, and earnings per share. There are methodologies that focus exclusively on financial value propositions. These don't always result in buying action because financial pain doesn't always translate into political pain or action.

Pain doesn't come from the business problem; pain comes from the political embarrassment *of the business problem.* Many things are not measured separately in accounting systems. They don't measure customer satisfaction or lost sales opportunities, many types of product quality or inefficiency or lost productivity, and employee morale. And they don't measure employee turnover in terms of writing off assets walking out the door. *If the pain or lost opportunity is not visible, then it's not embarrassing and it will not drive business buying activity to a close.*

> We had an opportunity at a railroad that wouldn't close or go away. They just kept on evaluating. One of the techniques to make the invisible more visible is to create a cost justification proposal of the cost of the lost benefits if they don't do anything. Then we take the return on investment of the project divided by twelve to determine how much it costs every month they don't take action.
>
> I asked my account manager, "Have we explained to them the cost of not doing business?"
>
> "Yes, we have," he replied. "We've shown them it will cost them twenty-five thousand dollars every month they don't do something."
>
> "And their reply?"
>
> "They said, 'Hey, we're a railroad. We've been losing money like this for hundreds of years. Nobody's ever gotten fired. The trains go in, the trains go out.'" In effect, it was a subsidized monopoly with no competition and no embarrassment for inefficiency.
>
> If the economic system doesn't create that embarrassment through competition, then the speed of commerce slows dramatically and so will your deal.

If we are to create urgency to generate or close business, we must creatively take the invisible costs and make them visible and politically painful. We must put a price tag on procrastination.

The client will only change when the cost of not changing exceeds the cost of changing. There must be a source of urgency, and political costs trump economic costs.

Political Benefits

While financial justifications are important as proof statements, risk reduction, and pain creators, quite often they ignore the impact of selling to emotional, political, cultural, and strategic benefits. We have found that where the issues are emotional or political issues of the top executives, cost justifications can often go out the window.

> Pain doesn't come from the business problem; pain comes from the political embarrassment of the business problem. The client will only change when their personal pain of not changing exceeds the pain of changing.

When I was in graduate school, one of my fellow students had been a financial analyst for Eastern Airlines. He told us a story of a memo that came down to the finance department that basically said, "Please cost justify the purchase of a corporate jet."

So they cranked the numbers and sent back a memo saying, "A corporate jet for a major airline makes no sense. We have already invested in our own airplanes; they fly higher, farther, faster, and safer than anything else. Based on a financial analysis, a corporate jet is not a good investment."

The day after they submitted their analysis, they received back exactly the same memo. The only difference was that the word "justify" had been underlined and the initials of the chairman were beside it.

"Oh, you meant 'justify' a corporate jet! We thought you meant 'cost justify' a corporate jet. Now we understand what you mean by 'justify.'"

Although significant cost reduction can be strategic, political, strategic, and emotional issues usually override cost justifications. Do we think that the merger activity between telephone companies, cellular companies, cable companies, and entertainment companies is being calculated to the fourth decimal place of return on investment out to the year 2050?

These are big numbers. They are both emotional and strategic. And the future isn't exactly foreseeable.

Strategic Benefits

Strategic benefits are the powerful issues on the mind of the CEO and other "C-level" executives. These include competitive advantage, market share, speed to market, survival, government regulation, litigation, global expansion, corporate culture, leadership, growth, and mergers and acquisitions.[8] They determine where the organization will be in the next five years.

If You Want Little Dollars, Solve Little Problems; If You Want Big Dollars, Solve Big Problems

A great example of solving big problems for big dollars involves one of our consulting clients, Mark Rodrigues of American Management Systems (AMS). Mark called on a bank in Europe. In the meeting were Mark, the business developer, along with the vice president of information technology and the vice president of finance.

Mark opened the meeting by asking, "What can we do for you?"

The information technology officer replied, "We have a fifty-thousand-dollar engagement for technical architecture consulting for an application we are starting to build."

Mark reacted. "Is that it? Fifty thousand dollars for technical architecture consulting? That's not what we do best. There are other product vendors that can do that as effectively as we can, for less money." But at that point, he began to drill down to the business problem. And the knife he used to peel back the onion to the business problem is a simple word. "Why?"

Every time you ask it, you dig deeper toward the real problem. "Why do you need the technical architecture?"

"Well, we have an application to develop, and we need to do it by January," said the IT manager.

"Why January?" asked the business developer.

"It's a government regulation," said the IT manager.

"Why is it a government regulation?"

"Derivatives control."

"Ah, derivatives control. Let me guess: You have one person trading highly leveraged derivatives, the whole bank is exposed, and nobody knows what he's doing. Am I right?"

"Precisely," said the VP of finance.

The business developer said, "So this is a *survival* issue to the bank, isn't it?"

"Exactly," said the VP of finance. Notice that Mark is now speaking *to the VP of finance* about a more important business problem.

"And since you're one of the lead banks in this country, this could be a survival issue for the country?" said the business developer.

"That's why it's a government regulation," said the VP of finance.

The business developer could have stopped there, but he actually went farther and higher up the value chain of business issues. "I understand you lost three hundred and fifty million dollars; people lost their jobs and went to jail; and it was all over the newspapers, right?"

"Right," said the VP of finance.

The business developer then went further and held up the annual report. "I read in your president's statement that he wants you to be one of the lead banks in Europe for multinational banking; is that correct?"

"You've done your homework," said the VP of finance. "It's an important goal."

The business developer asked, "Do you think he's going to be satisfied if we tell him that we built a system to make us compliant? We're just like all the other banks, we're compliant. Instead, how would you like to have the best derivatives control system in Europe, to be able to draw multinational banks to you and gain competitive advantage?"

"That's exactly what we want," said the VP of finance.

"That's exactly what we are qualified to do for you," said Mark.

The initial inquiry was for fifty thousand dollars. When they signed the deal, it was for five million dollars, which may only be a starter kit for several years of the same level of billing.

Mark was effective in "peeling back the onion" of pain. The deeper he cut to the strategic business problem, the higher he went on the value chain and the bigger the deal grew, as well as their competitive advantage.

If bulk steel is a dollar a pound, when it's made into automobile parts it's five dollars a pound, when it's made into surgical scalpels it's a thousand dollars a pound. It is based on perceived value.

Strategic solutions yield better prices than operational or commodity solutions; emotional and political problems drive buying activity more than logical ones.

Only after gaining a greater understanding of the client's problems and process can we decide whether they are a qualified prospect—the next step in the R.A.D.A.R. process.

Summary: Key 1—Link Solutions to *Pain* (or *Gain*)

● Gaining confession of the client's need is the heart of consultative selling.

● Get the client talking by using questions that begin with "who, what, why, where, and when."

● Understanding client needs is not the same as understanding client requirements.

● Don't assume that a committee made up of multiple buyers really speaks with one voice.

● Personal agenda items must be uncovered.

● The simple "so what" test is critical to linking your benefits to the client's needs.

● Identify operational, cultural, financial, political, and strategic pain.

● Sell strategic benefits to strategic buyers, tactical benefits to technical buyers.

● Strategic benefits trump technical and tactical benefits.

● The deeper you cut to the strategic business problem, the higher you will rise on the value chain, along with your pricing.

For a set of wall posters containing the chapter summaries and quotes from this book—please contact: Nautilus Press, Inc., 4279 Roswell Road, Suite 102-282, Atlanta, GA 30342; info@nautiluspress.com; ph. 1-800-324-4582.

CHAPTER 8

Key 2—Qualify the *Prospect*

Key Questions
- *Is this good business for anyone?*
- *Is this a winnable opportunity for us?*
- *How does it compare to the rest of my opportunities?*

One of the keys to success in business development is picking winnable battles. But how you qualify a prospect depends on how many opportunities you have and how many resources you have available. The salesperson who has a full pipeline and more prospects than he or she can pursue qualifies in a much different manner than a salesperson at a lesser-known company or a new territory just trying to get in the game. *Consequently, there is no one mathematical process for qualifying prospects.*

> How you qualify depends on how many opportunities you have and how many resources you have available.

Qualification Is Relative
In addition to assessing your chances of winning, other qualification questions should include, "How does this opportunity compare with the rest of my opportunities?" and "What resources would it require?" The answer is unique and different to every company and will vary from territory to territory.

The new account manager with nothing going works on opportunities that others would walk away from. With a busy pipeline, veterans prefer to win or lose early. Moreover, since each person's territory and pipeline are quite different, what is qualified for one rep may not be the best use of team-selling resources for the region or the firm as a whole.

Qualifying vs. Positive Mental Attitude

One of the obstacles for qualifying is also one of the essentials for selling: a positive mental attitude. If you didn't have it, you wouldn't start each day and wouldn't be in the business of selling. It is what enables a salesperson to start with a blank piece of paper and produce million-dollar quotas. It is what enables hunters to overcome obstacles and turn defeats into victories.

> This is the way qualification should be done—weighing the resources required to stay in versus your chances of winning.

If you look at your experience unemotionally, you'll see that the number of times miracle turnarounds happen (and they make great bar stories) compared to the number of times you actually pour money into losing causes tells us that maybe what is needed is a less emotional process of qualification. But where is the line between qualification and quitting? Where is the line between a positive mental attitude and the rookie trait of over optimistic "happy ears"? A *Fortune* magazine article on "Why CEOs Fail"[9] says one of the warning signs of executive denial is a background in sales or marketing. A positive mental attitude is essential to selling, but as we have said, *hope is not a strategy*.

The first key qualifying question for anyone should be, "Will this business happen for anyone at all?" Experience has shown that many evaluations end with no buying activity whatsoever. When evaluations stall or fail to happen at all, one of two things is usually missing: either there is not a business problem of great enough magnitude or urgency, or the project lacks political sponsorship to see it through the maze to completion. And with no pain or power, this deal is not going to happen in our lifetime.

The second key question becomes, "Is this a good opportunity for us?" In up to one-fourth of these evaluations, the vendor is already informally selected before the process begins.

Column B and C in the Buyer's Matrix— Before It Even Starts

We talked before about why the customer might want to keep you in the game when you're not winning.

Why would someone conduct a competitive evaluation when they already know who they want? There are many reasons and all are political:

● The client may need to show due diligence.
● They may not legally be allowed to sole source.
● They may need to validate their decision.
● They may need to educate themselves about other issues.
● They may need to create buy-in from a project team by letting them participate in the evaluation.

Make sure you are not the stalking horse in these situations. If you get an unsolicited RFP on your desk and you didn't write it, there is a chance that someone else did. If that's the case, you are merely column B or C in that person's due diligence matrix, but you may not know it until too late.

About Budgets

One of the indicators traditionally used by salespeople to determine the viability of the opportunity is, "Is the money in the budget?" To some salespeople, this is a binary question. No budget, no prospect. But if the offering is strategic enough, budgets may only be an indicator.

Money in the budget indicates management thought there was a big enough business problem to commit funds for the coming year. The CEO and other chief officers are always planning ahead of budget and can often spend off of the current budget. If there is no money in the budget to solve the business problem, that means one of two things: (1) get high enough in the organization to someone who can spend money off budget, or (2) sell it this year to get it in the budget for next year.

In either case, it is a longer sales cycle. You'll need to get higher in the organization, and the political risks are greater. But that doesn't mean you walk away from it. The most important emotional and strategic issues are quite often not budgeted. They arise between budget cycles. Or opportunities that have a rapid enough return on investment may pay for themselves in the current year. Or if the sponsor is powerful enough, budgets may only be a guideline.

The next budget question leads into politics. "Whose budget is the money in?" If the money is in someone's budget who opposes you, you have a problem. It's the golden rule of budgeting—the one who has the gold makes the rules. Not exactly, but they do have more power.

The next issue to be examined is financial stability. Do they have the ability to pay? Money can be in the budget, but one bad quarter for a manufacturing company can stop all capital purchases. A low stock price could produce an acquisition or an austerity program.

Moreover, there may be other threats to the project. You may have a return on investment to justify the project, but there may not be enough cash or budget money, or other priorities will prevail.

Demand Creation vs. Demand Reaction

One of our consulting clients, a management consultant, illustrated the difference between the qualification process for consultants and product sales: "We often stimulate demand where the client hasn't seen it yet. We find business problems that have not become evaluations yet and turn them into engagements. If we qualified hard, we wouldn't propose anywhere." This is why salespeople in consulting are called business developers.

The questions in this model are: "Will the pain drive buying activity?" and "Can we find a power sponsor?" This is because the biggest competitor to demand-creation selling is "no action," where the client evaluates and buys nothing from anyone.

Intangible Qualifications

There are also strategic and intangible reasons that override a logical analysis as to why you pursue a particular opportunity. It may be a brand-name customer. You may want to penetrate an industry or country. You may want to prevent a competitor from getting a toehold. Or you may want to take a marginally profitable opportunity yourself to gain a toehold into the account.

Another key question in qualification is, "Will the business be profitable?" Unfortunately, most salespeople are not measured on profitability; they are measured on revenue. Consequently they don't ask this important question enough because it's not on their agenda.

Finally, "Will this business result in a satisfied client?" If it doesn't, you may get this piece of business and inoculate the client and the client's executives from doing business with you again anywhere. Unfortunately, most salespeople are measured on revenue rather than customer satisfaction and repeat sales. But don't underestimate the personal impact of signing bad business on your reputation with network peers—it can be career limiting.

Buy Another Card?

Account qualification isn't always a binary "go" or "bi-go." It's more like playing poker. In one type of poker, we put a dollar in the pot and we get a card up and a card down. Initially, we don't know much, and the first round of betting is not very expensive, perhaps a quarter. As the game proceeds, someone pairs up and suddenly the price of poker goes up.

It's going to cost us more to stay in this game, which must be weighed against our odds of winning. This is the way qualification should be done—weighing the resources in time and talent required versus our chances of winning. The earlier and tougher the qualifying is, the more effective it is.

Like poker, eventually you will have five cards out and ten dollars in the pot, at which time your thinking changes. Instead of focusing on the *opportunity*, you now think about the *investment* you have and how you can't let that money go to waste. So you stay in until the last card, but the last card doesn't cost a quarter or even a dollar. It costs twenty dollars, because there is no end to the betting and no limits.

With a busy pipeline, veterans prefer to win early or lose early.

After a certain amount of investment, the deal is managing you—sucking up resources. In hindsight, you wish you had never engaged in the first place. You must have a process for telling *in advance* which deals you should get in and which you shouldn't.

If you have relative strengths, there is almost no deal you can't win with enough effort. But at what cost and at what risk? The worst-case scenario is to commit significant resources and finish second. There are no silver medals in selling and, unlike race car driving, there is not even any lap money for leading the race.

Your qualification process must include at several points a "go," a "no-go," and an option to "buy another card," depending on how expensive that card is.

We may qualify out because of any of the following reasons:

● We can't solve their pain well.
● We have no access to power.
● The decision-making process doesn't favor us.
● We don't have the resources for adequate pursuit.
● We have better opportunities elsewhere.

But having picked a battle we can win, we need now to win the battle we have picked by winning the hearts of the decision makers.

Summary: Key 2—Qualify the *Prospect*

● Pick winnable battles based on analysis rather than emotion.

● There is no one mathematical process for qualifying prospects.

● How you qualify is relative to how many opportunities you have and how many resources you have available.

● The most important emotional and strategic issues are quite often not budgeted.

● Ask yourself if the business will be profitable.

● Ask yourself if it will result in a satisfied client.

● Qualifying isn't quitting.

● A positive mental attitude is an essential for selling but often an obstacle for qualifying.

● Most sales people don't ask the tough questions because it will spoil a perfectly good forecast.

For a set of wall posters containing the chapter summaries and quotes from this book— please contact: Nautilus Press, Inc., 4279 Roswell Road, Suite 102-282, Atlanta, GA 30342; info@nautiluspress.com; ph. 1-800-324-4582.

CHAPTER 9

Key 3—Build Competitive *Preference*

Without competitors there would be no need for strategy.

Kenichi Ohmae
The Mind of the Strategist

Key Questions

- *Can we win?*
- *How do we win?*
- *If each person had to vote today, would they recommend us?*
- *What are our differentiators?*
- *How would the competition defeat us?*

Preference is the degree to which a recommendor or influencer from a buying committee will oppose you or help you win. How do you build it? First of all, it's important to understand the range of preferences that are possible in the complex sale. We have defined a scale of preference that runs from neutral in the middle, to *open and accepting*, to a point where individuals begin *supporting* you in your efforts. The key question here is, "If they had to vote today, would they vote for us?"

Positive preference rises to the next level where they are *disclosing* to you information you need about their company and its politics that will help you win. The highest level of preference is *trust*, an unexpressed feeling of "Whatever you're selling, we're buying."

Negative preference ranges from indifferent and skeptical to challenging your statements, to open opposition, and finally to overt hostility. You should decide if a person has too much preference for the competition for us to overcome. If they are an unconvertible opponent, then the information we provide to try to change their preference may be going straight into the hands of the competition.

Positioning—The Art of Saying It First

A psychological principle popularized by Ries and Trout[10] taught us that it is many times easier to help someone make up their mind in the first place than it is to change it. At a certain stage, baby animals "imprint" on the first living thing they see as its mother. A baby duck can imprint on a Saint Bernard.

Think of wet and hard cement. The first to sculpt a vision of leadership, advantage, or solution in the prospect's head will gain greater mind-share than the followers who must counter-position themselves.

It's not just a matter of making a good first impression; you have to make a good first impression *first*. The best time to do this is obviously in the first call or in the needs assessment—so get there first. What you thought was early in the sale wasn't early enough.

Benefits Mapping

Building preference with an individual is a function of fundamental one-on-one selling skills: personality, credibility, persuasiveness, linkage, and alignment. The client wants to know how your capabilities and solution will benefit them personally, as well as their organization.

Building preference in an opportunity is a matter of building positive mind-share first with key influencers, then getting others to jump on the bandwagon as preference momentum builds. At the account level it means delivering what was sold, making your sponsors look good, and building relationships from rapport to trust.

Competitive Selling—Stay On the Ethical High Ground

The effective salesperson, however, can influence the issues, the politics, and the process without ever mentioning the competitor's name. As the evaluation continues and the prospect can't differentiate, you may be asked to compare your solutions.

How quickly and openly you can discuss competitive issues depends on your relationship with the individual prospect, your competitive position, the stage of the sales cycle, and which region of which country you are in. In the United States, comparative advertising has been around for many years, but such comparisons are illegal in other countries.

Without mentioning the competition, however, you can build rapport before the competition arrives. You can suggest questions and issues the client should ask everyone; you can suggest requirements of all vendors; you can stress your unique capabilities and differentiators; and you can suggest steps in the evaluation cycle for all vendors. Of course, the issues and steps you suggest are those that focus on your strengths and the competitor's weaknesses, but you have shaped the battlefield without ever mentioning the competitor.

Counter-Strategy

The best sales strategists, like the best pool players, chess players, and generals, look at their opportunity through their competitor's eyes. "If I were my competitor, how would I defeat me?" *This is critical thinking, not negative thinking.* It allows us to anticipate the competitor's actions, predict them, and neutralize them before they are able to execute. Doing this requires a victory of critical thinking over positive mental attitude. Real confidence comes from a plan that has been *tested* and will win. Hope doesn't drive strategy; information drives strategy.

In the movie *Patton*, the Germans appointed one of their brightest young captains to study Patton and predict his behavior. He did so very effectively; unfortunately, his supervisors chose to ignore his advice. At the Battle of El Guettar, as Rommel's troops were advancing, Patton was looking through his binoculars and said, "Rommel, I read your book." Patton had studied Rommel's armored tactics, anticipated his approach, and defeated his strategy by being able to analyze his own plan through the eyes of the competitor.

Likewise, the best competitive salespeople can anticipate a competitor's strategy and neutralize it before it happens.

Controlling the Point of Entry

Successful hunters use many competitive tactics to establish preference by individuals and groups. The first step in establishing control of an opportunity is establishing the political point of entry.

Many salespeople don't even try to control this important first step. Early in sales training we are taught to be responsive to the customer. When someone from their client's office calls, they answer right back. The problem is that frequently a lower level project team member is assigned to gather information. One thing is for sure, as soon as you contact them, they tell you, "I'm the decision maker. You can only talk to me." You are now trapped.

Some salespeople work hard and fast upon learning of buying activity to see that their first point of entry is at the executive level. It is obviously easier if they are already a client or if they had used your services elsewhere. There are means of political navigation that are more effective than the direct call, which we'll discuss later. But there is a brief window early, in non-government accounts, while there's forgiveness and before the rules of engagement are established, where you might gain access.

A call to the executive to determine whether there is viable buying activity going on often yields some very interesting results. In some cases, the executive says, "No, there's no buying activity going on here. Nothing is authorized." This executive just saved you weeks and months of activity.

Or the executive may say, "Yes, there is some interest," but the name of the person he or she gives you as the decision maker isn't the name of the person who is calling you. You may have headed into a political cul-de-sac.

Having established this channel of communication, never give it up; always leave a good reason to call this executive back. "Do you mind if I keep you appraised of how the project is going? And by the way, when we do the needs assessment, we'd like to spend some time with you to understand what the strategic objectives are for this project."

The best consulting firms are effective at making sure their point of entry is top-down, because if they're going to change culture and process, it's the only approach that will work. After some period of time, however, if the client has contacted you and you've been unable to establish a different point of entry, you have to respond to the prospect or you will appear unresponsive.

At that point you have to change your navigation path to bottom-up for this opportunity because it's all you can get. But remember that once they become a client, you need a process and a plan to move up to top-down selling before the second evaluation breaks out.

Rapport and Bonding

The first buying decision an individual prospect makes is about the salesperson. An essential process for building preference is obviously establishing rapport and building bonds. This is where face-to-face selling, personality, and chemistry are essential. This is also the subject area of much of the sales literature, because for a simple sale, building bonds with a single buyer is the biggest step in the sale.

In fact, Dale Carnegie's initial book, *How to Win Friends and Influence People*, was the first approach to making more of a science out of this art. It is still a top-selling book, and very sound in its advice. Building bonds runs the range of eye contact, handshake, use of humor, mutuality, learning someone's name, understanding their problems, and listening. The newer techniques of neuro-linguistic programming help salespeople align body language, level and speed of voice, familiarity, and humor to that of the buyer.

Initially building rapport leads to credibility, which leads to trust. We have to build this bridge quickly and effectively because we can only push as much competitive armor across that bridge as the relationship can sustain. And we will only get as much vital competitive and political information in return as the relationship will bear.

You must build this bridge of rapport to the point of supporting and disclosure, to where they want you to win because they think it is best for their organization. Talking about personal or competitive issues before you have established rapport is unprofessional and can be catastrophic. You will be perceived as negative and pushy. And you will only receive as much competitive information and information about their buying process as they trust your solution is best for their organization.

It Starts From The Heart

If the bridge of bonds is not built, or breached through insincerity, lack of conviction, or poor credibility, it becomes an open drawbridge. You can have the world's greatest product, solution, and company, but it will all fall into the water. You can lose a good message through a bad messenger.

I had a sales representative who for two years generated very little business. Normally, we wouldn't allow someone unproductive to work for us for so long, but he was doing so many things right, it took us a while to figure out why he was not successful. In the end it was chemistry.

He was selling to government buyers but didn't like the people he met there. None of us is a good enough actor to hide it. Selling starts from the heart—if we don't like them, they won't like us. And they will find a million logical reasons to justify buying from someone else. This salesperson went on to a very successful career in another company with a different type of clientele.

Influence the Issues

"The customer is always right," Stew Leonard, the dairy store owner, taught us in Tom Peters' book *Thriving on Chaos* [11]. But what if the customer is multiple people who don't agree with each other? Who is "right" is the individual client with the most power or the best business case. In complex solutions made up of things they've never bought before, the "customer" may not have a clear picture of what they want and will rely on vendors and consultants to educate them.

Defining requirements is an inexact art. If a salesperson takes a list of requirements as tablets of stone to be met or not, he or she underestimates his or her ability to steer the buying criteria. The best time to have done this is while you were delivering the previous piece of business. The next best time is during the needs analysis while the cement is still wet.

A consultative salesperson can suggest capabilities that should be considered (obviously those things we do well) for buying criteria.

In some cases, what the inexperienced prospect "wants" isn't what the prospect needs. Your task is to either reeducate them and reshape their vision, or failing that, consider whether the client can be successful at all if they don't consider these issues. If they don't consider the environmental issues of change management and process reengineering surrounding the product, you may not want this business under those conditions.

A vice president of American Management Systems (AMS) was in an evaluation for a major federal government department. The demo was scripted by the IT department, and it was obvious it was the competitor's script. She looked at the situation, assessed it, and concluded that AMS couldn't win under the circumstances.

During the demonstration, she kept bringing up other issues such as implementation, risk management, intergovernmental accounting, workflow, and business processes—areas her company was especially good at, since it has a large market share of the federal market for financial systems. Initially, the client got upset that she wasn't following the script and asked her to leave.

But later on, when they were on the risk curve thinking about how they were going to implement anything and focused on the change management business process issues, the seeds of truth began to sprout. They began to realize she knew what she was talking about and they were the more important issues. They not only invited AMS back in, but they specified her in the contract, which was an initial nineteen-million-dollar engagement.

Steer the Process

The next step is to influence the evaluation process. This means suggesting the client add steps that will highlight your strengths or the competitor's weaknesses, or take out steps that require lots of resources.

One of our clients was in competition for a financial services system for a major West Coast bank. He was competing with a small firm he knew very well since he used to work there. He suggested to the client they add a benchmark pilot, which is normally a resource-intensive proof step usually avoided if at all possible. However, he knew the competitor was limited in resources, and some of their functionality was not currently available. By raising the bar, he invested time and resources to do a proof exercise. The competitor wouldn't match the effort, and he won the engagement, which is now a major partnership for millions of dollars a year.

Identify the Influencers

As early and as delicately as possible, identify the more powerful influencers and what parts people will play in the sales cycle.

You must commit resources and win these votes early. These individuals have a higher return on invested time if it's invested early because they will lead the rest as well as tell you how to win.

You will then need a process for political navigation and the skill of strategic literacy—how to get to executives and what to say when you get there.

Win Their Hearts—Before It Starts

By the way, the best way to have won their hearts is in the *last* sale by having exceeded expectations and by having stayed in touch. But then that's account management. If you haven't already done that, it's a little late now.

You need to have as many powerful people and issues in your favor as possible entering the crucible, because the intensity and pace will pick up as the client's committee nears the crucial decision-making stage.

Summary: Key 3—*Build Competitive Preference*

● The first step in controlling an opportunity is establishing the political point of entry.

● The highest level of preference is trust.

● Build positive mind-share by positioning first with key influencers.

● Positioning is the art of saying it first.

● Once you establish a channel of communication with the executive, always leave a good reason to call back.

● The ideal point of entry is top-down.

● People buy from people; establish a bridge of rapport and build bonds.

● You'll only get as much vital competitive and political information as the relationship will bear.

● You can lose a good message through a bad messenger.

● Win their hearts before it starts.

● It is many times easier to help someone make up their mind in the first place than it is to change it.

● What you thought was early in the sale probably isn't early enough!

For a set of wall posters containing the chapter summaries and quotes from this book—please contact: Nautilus Press, Inc., 4279 Roswell Road, Suite 102-282, Atlanta, GA 30342; info@nautiluspress.com; ph. 1-800-324-4582.

CHAPTER 10

Key 4—Determine the Decision-Making *Process*

> *The single most important talent in selling profes-*
> *sional services is the ability to understand the*
> *purchasing process from the clients' perspective.*
>
> David Maister
> *Managing the Professional Service Firm*

Key Questions

- ■ *How do* they *think they will decide? In whose opinion?*
- ■ *How do* you *think they will decide?*
- ■ *What part will each person play?*
- ■ *When will they decide?*
- ■ *What is the approval process?*

Right Count, Wrong Process—A Fatal Blind Spot

I once asked our salesperson, "How are we doing?"

He said, "Great, we're winning seven to five."

I said, "Terrific. Sounds like it's our business. When do they vote?"

"They vote tomorrow."

We lost. There were seven people on the project team from manufacturing, all of whom preferred us, two people from accounting, and three people from the IT department. Our problem was that they *voted by department.* We lost the IT department and accounting and won manufacturing; we lost two departments to one.

What could have been done differently? We could have focused more time and attention on one of the other two departments, knowing that we needed one of them to win. Perhaps two out of three in IT would have done it for us.

We also could have expanded scope to add new solutions and capabilities to draw more people into the departments where we were losing in hopes of creating preference for us for our capability in those departments. So perhaps we could have won accounting five to two.

Perhaps there is even another entire department that could be brought into the decision-making process to our advantage. We could have gone to our friends in the manufacturing department and said, "Based on this decision-making process, we won't win and you will not get the system you want," creating a power struggle over the decision-making process itself.

"This is a manufacturing solution, why do accounting and IT get to vote? They're staff departments. You own the business problem. You have to manufacture the goods. Why don't you change the decision-making process where you pick the product with their advice?"

Another strategy could have been to stall altogether, knowing that if they voted now, we wouldn't win. Perhaps in time people would leave the project team, issues might change, competitors can shoot themselves in the foot, or we may increase our capabilities. All sorts of things can happen, all of which beat losing now by just letting things happen.

Nothing is more important in driving an accurate strategy than understanding the client's decision-making process. Bad information about the decision-making process led to a poor strategy, overconfidence, and defeat. But knowing the decision-making process could drive a change in strategy to stay in the game and change the issues.

In a simple sale with a single buyer, you would find the pain, link your solution to it, create preference, and then close. In the complex sale, however, the decision-making process of multiple buyers often becomes convoluted when they can't reach a consensus. This is because project teams typically have a well-defined *evaluation* process but not a tie-breaking *decision-making* process when they don't all agree.

> "They don't decide how to decide until they can't decide."

"Buy-In"

The term "vote" is quite often thrown about in project teams. This is because one of the reasons for having evaluations is to create participation and, therefore, "buy-in" among project team members who must implement a solution.

Participation and buy-in, however, are different from consensus. Top management wants people to feel like they had their say, even if they didn't get their way. When power struggles break out and emotions and politics erupt, quite often the bullets are still flying as the project starts. There are winners and losers, and indeed quite often saboteurs.

Algebraic Democracy

What happens in many cases is what I have termed algebraic democracy. Most people involved have a vote of some sort, but some people's votes may count more than others. Some people's votes count x, some count $5x$, and there may be some $10x$ votes. In some companies there may be one person whose vote outweighs everyone.

> Participation and buy-in is different from consensus.

Whose Vote Counts?

In some situations people get a *straw vote*. Their recommendations are taken in, but they aren't counted. They are simply qualitative recommendations, and the decision makers will take them and pick a vendor. Knowing this decision-making process creates a much different strategy and resource allocation.

Two-Tiered Decisions

A regional airline was buying a suite of enterprise financial systems. While meeting with the project team leader, we got every out-of-control signal in the book. It was obvious to us at this point we were not winning, and we were prepared to walk (which wasn't far considering they resided in our building).

Our team and the project leader were headed to the parking lot at the end of the day when the project leader said something that created new information that lead to a new objective and a new strategy. He said, "Oh, by the way, the decision-making process is this: The project team will actually pick two vendors and then the top four executives in the company will pick the winner." New information, a new objective, and a new strategy. This is a *two-tiered decision*. We don't need to win at this point. All we need to do is stay alive. If we can make it to the final two, which we felt we could, perhaps issues would change.

That is exactly what happened. They said, "You bring your president; they'll bring their president. We'll meet with four of our vice presidents." We prepared well for this meeting. We came in with a story tailored to the airline industry focusing on their business issues: hub productivity, measuring revenues and costs per passenger mile, and success stories from airlines around the world who were our clients.

Our president, Bill Graves, was knowledgeable in areas of investment banking. On a personal level, they liked wine and our president was an expert on wine and had a cellar of thousands of bottles, some of which he shared. We offered to locate an on-site support person and begin strengthening our office in that town. We connected on all fronts.

Our competitor's chairman wrote their product. Their strength came from its technical sophistication. So when they met with these executives, what do you think they discussed? Technical issues, feeds and speeds, bits and bytes. Their words hit 'em in the forehead and fell to the floor with no effect. The issues had all changed with the new players.

The significance of these stories is that to the untrained eye, the decision-making process can seem arbitrary or convoluted. But the more you can understand about the decision-making process, the more effective your strategy and resource allocation will be.

> Speed and accuracy of information drive speed and accuracy of strategy which drive competitive advantage.

Demystifying the Decision-Making Process

One problem is that the client often doesn't know their own decision-making process . They usually have a well-defined information-gathering process they hope will lead to a consensus. This only happens in Japan, where the process takes a very long time.

As the client reaches the crucible without a consensus, politics erupt and multimillion-dollar deals can turn around in a day. You could ask six people inside the organization about the decision-making process and get eight opinions—and all could be wrong. A salesperson must have a greater understanding of how the decision might be reached than even the client does.

Since a committee is a group of people, each with a separate set of pains, preferences, power, and each playing different parts, how could one strategy and message fit them all? As politicians have done for years, you need to break the committee down into its component parts and count the votes. You then need to come up with separate strategies and messages for each important participant. You must break your strategy down into more granular tactics at the individual stakeholder level. The more you can understand about the decision-making process, the more effective your strategy and resource allocation will be.

Parts and Roles—A Purchasing Polyglot

There are many terms from a variety of sales literature that are useful in describing the various roles in a complex sale, but these address only part of the problem. A decision-making process is made up of events and people. So we sometimes use the term *part* interchangeably with *process* to describe an individual role in the decision.

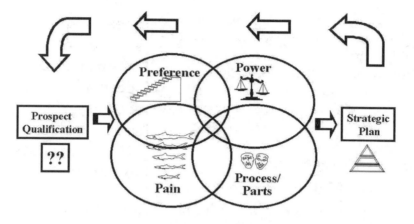

Stakeholder Analysis

Figure 10-1 *To arrive at a four-level sales plan, you must analyze each stakeholder based upon their pain (or gain), preference for you, their power, and the part they will play in the decision-making process.*

The parts that each person plays in a group decision were first identified by Tom Bonoma.[12] The vernacular of other authors has added to the vocabulary of selling. Who are the *decision makers, approvers, gatekeepers, and influencers?* Miller and Heiman[13] identified *economic buyers, technical buyers, and coaches* in the mid-eighties. Are there *potential influencers* we can bring in on our side? Are some players *nonparticipants* for some reason?

The stakeholder analysis in Figure 10 helps add greater definition to these general terms. For example, the term "coach" in common practice is used to describe someone who is trying to help us win. But we have all actually had "coaches" who killed us—people who tried to help us win but actually cost us the business. Why? Because "coach," as commonly used, is an indicator of *preference, not of power.* In some cases you can have people who like you, but who are so disliked in their own organizations, they can actually set you back.

When Will They Decide? Or— Will They Buy in Our Lifetime?

A scenario repeated over and over is that of a sales manager en route to an account who asks the salesperson, "You have it on the forecast that they'll buy by the end of the quarter. Why do you say that?"

"Well, I've got the bonus and a trip. They have to buy at the end of the quarter," the salesperson explains.

The now-worried sales manager says, "Well, that's certainly *your* reason for why they should buy by the end of the quarter. Does *the client* have one?"

"I don't know. Let's ask them when we get there."

The obvious question in the sales managers mind is, "If you haven't identified this important piece of information, why are we going to the client with the manager in tow?"

While meeting with their client, the sales manager asks, "Mr. or Ms. Prospect, what bad thing will happen if you don't make a decision by the end of the quarter?"

The client stares back with incredulity and says, "Well, nothing. I suppose we'll just keep on looking."

This salesperson may now be envisioning new horizons on their career path!

Publicly-owned companies who need quarterly results try to drive their client's buying cycle timing to the selling cycle of the vendor. In the absence of a true source of urgency, too often salespeople resort to price or discounts in order to create urgency.

"Mr. or Ms. Prospect, we've announced a 6.2 percent price increase. We'd hate to see you buy the same proposal later at a higher price, so we really do need to get your business in by the end of the quarter to secure this price," says the salesperson.

To which the seasoned buyer says, "Gee, a price increase at the end of the quarter to close business—what a novel marketing approach. You're the first one in here today doing that. There were four yesterday."

Not only is this technique predictable, but after months and months of building value for our solution, you have now commodified *yourself*. You have turned it from value to price in order to close business at the end of the quarter. And once you've offered a discount to close business, you have announced what kind of vendor you are, and the only question now is the price. Let the games begin.

Commodification of opportunities at the end of a quarter drives sales managers crazy and can actually significantly impact the shareholder value of companies.

Sources of Urgency— The Foundation of Forecast Accuracy

Business that keeps sliding backwards in time and won't close usually means that one of two things is missing: Either the *pain* is not great enough to cause them to buy now, or there is not enough political *power* driving the opportunity to a close. Pain or power is missing, and that should have been detected earlier in the sales cycle. If you had a rich pipeline, you might have disqualified this account early. With a thin pipeline, you may still pursue it in hopes of creating urgency or gaining access to power.

Usually a pain or business problem must be great enough to cause the business to close now, or it may not happen at all. The best salespeople detect and close on the *client's* pain or opportunity, not their own. Forecasts will also be more accurate if we are closing on the client's source of urgency rather than our own.

In negotiation, power lies in alternatives. If the client knows that you have a deadline, they have the power. If you know they have a deadline, or an urgent business problem, you have the power. If you know you are in a winning position going into the negotiation, you don't have to give away the store.

The source of urgency from the client's side may include:

- Obsolescence of the current system
- Government regulation
- Seasonality
- Management edict
- Personal agenda
- New product rollout
- New plant being built
- Project deadline
- A major piece of lost business
- Elections
- Changing technology

Some of these business problems are more urgent than others. As we illustrated with the railroad example cited earlier, financial returns alone won't excite people to buy. Problems with dates attached to them, along with political exposure for making or missing those dates, have the highest urgency, especially if it means exposure for powerful people.

Regarding powerful people, a consultative salesperson must know how to recognize who has power, how to build influence with them, and how to borrow it for access. Getting powerful people on your side early will give you greater leverage as the client organization approaches the decision and will provide greater assurance that a commitment will be made at all.

> In negotiation, power lies in alternatives. If the client knows you have a deadline, *they* have the power. If you know they have a deadline or an urgent business problem, *you* have the power.

Summary: Key 4—Determine The Decision-Making *Process*

● Nothing is more important to driving an accurate strategy than understanding your client's decision-making process.

● Project teams typically have a well-defined evaluation process but not a well-defined decision-making process.

● In the law of algebraic democracy, some people's votes count more than others.

● Know who gets a straw vote and who gets a real one.

● A salesperson must understand how a decision will be reached even more clearly than the client does.

● You must also understand the approval process once you've been chosen.

● Analyze each stakeholder based on pain, preference, power, and the part he or she plays in the decision-making process.

● Don't resort to price or discounts to create a sense of urgency.

● Commodification is avoided if you close on the client's pain or time frame, not your own.

● In negotiation, power lies in alternatives, weakness in deadlines.

For a set of wall posters containing the chapter summaries and quotes from this book— please contact: Nautilus Press, Inc., 4279 Roswell Road, Suite 102-282, Atlanta, GA 30342; info@nautiluspress.com; ph. 1-800-324-4582.

CHAPTER 11

Key 5—Sell to *Power*

> *Every company has two organizational structures: The formal one is written on the charts; the other is the living relationship of the men and women in the organization.*
>
> Harold Geneen, CEO, ITT
> *Managing*

Key Questions

■ *Are there powerful people helping us?*

■ *Who do we need to be calling on to earn this business?*

■ *Who influences them?*

■ *Who else might become involved?*

■ *Who is helping our competitors?*

We may be equal in the eyes of the Lord and the law, but not when it comes to buying decisions of major purchases. Not all votes are equal in a complex sale. Large organizations are not democracies, and some votes are bigger than others. The impact of politics on business decision making has been recognized by business writers since the early 1960s; it's been around much longer than that.

Often committees can't reach a consensus and don't have a clear process for how to resolve the impasse. If political activity hasn't already been at work, it erupts now.

Some people don't like politics and think it's not fair. And politics does have its negative aspect. All you need to do is read the paper each day to see political tactics being used for personal gain. That's the dark side of power and the negative definition most people give to politics. But politics does have a positive dimension—it is the way people with different points of view resolve their differences without fighting. The U.S. Constitution has stood the test of time for more than two hundred years (and only broke down into fighting once).

Political activity in business decisions is there and it's real. You can either ignore it and whine about it, or learn to recognize it and manage it. People who don't know what power is, how to recognize it, how to build it, and how to use it will be perpetual victims rather than victors in the complex sale.

The Shadow Organization Chart

Power is invisible. You can see the titles on the door, but as Henry Mintzberg described, within every organization is an invisible power structure that has little to do with organizational lines.[14]

Not only is power invisible, it's dynamic. It changes daily. People gain and lose power on a regular basis. And it is not a universal halo; it is vectored between individuals. We may have power with one person, no power with another, and negative power with another.

Negative power comes from ethical or performance problems, cultural misalignment, or poor people skills. It's hard to believe, but there are actually some votes you may not want because if they are for you, others will automatically be against you.

Why Do You Need to Know About Power?

1. You need to know how to *identify* power and *who has it* inside your prospect account. Your strategy should then allocate time to those people and *secure their support* early in the process. They will lead others and leverage your time.

2. You need to use these same tools to *build influence* with them and preference for you.

3. If you don't have power, *you can borrow it*. You can borrow it from one person to gain access to or information about another, or to have them influence someone else.

4. You need influence *to build your own personal network* inside your own companies to get things done for the client and inside your own industry to develop your own personal network.

The problem a salesperson faces is that you come into an account, and it's as if you have a freeze frame or snapshot of a motion picture that has been going on for two to five years. You have to figure out quickly who the powerful people are, what the plot is, and what's happened so far so you can project what might happen in the future. From the very first meeting, you need to start asking not only needs and process questions, but questions about political power so you can inventory who has power and discover where to invest your time.

The traditional source of power for many years was formal or positional authority, which comes from someone's title and place on the organization chart. But as power was studied more closely, and as management techniques began to change, more attention was paid to personal power or influence.

Some of the best books on this important topic are Jeffrey Pfeffer of Stanford University's *Managing with Power*, Bradford and Cohen's *Influence Without Authority*, and the London School of Economics' Charles Handy's *Understanding Organizations*.

Power Tools—Sources of Influence

Influence means getting things done through other people *without the use of authority*. Queen Elizabeth has titles; Princess Diana had influence.

Stephen Covey, in *The Seven Habits of Highly Effective People*, said it well: "We build emotional bank accounts with each other."[15] Other business writers have called it "social capital." How do people influence others without authority? How do people earn other people's trust? In our workshops, clients often come up with more than fifty different sources of influence and the power that flows from them.

Reciprocity—Favors and Gratitude

Effective sales leaders constantly make deposits and build networks of people inside their organizations and industry who help them get things done for the client (as well as themselves).

When Doug MacIntyre was a sales rep, he created a series of cards with a tiger theme. They were simple notes thanking someone for the extra effort on the proposal, for solving a client's problem, or traveling overnight to get to a presentation. (It's the hundreds of little things people do to help make a team better.)

These were simple acknowledgments, but to add value to them, they were good for one free drink. Once a year, he had a party where people could bring the coupons and cash them in at a local bar.

People never brought the coupons. Ten years later, where do you think those coupons were? On people's walls and cubicles. Ten years later, where do you think this salesperson was? He was CEO of the company. He built his own personal network simply by acknowledging the hundreds of people who helped him be successful.

You don't actually keep score, but you must make deposits before you can make withdrawals. But some people never seem to figure this out.

I worked with a salesperson who had been a successful performer for two consecutive years, but when a management position opened up in front of him, I couldn't promote him.

One by one, the technical product salespeople slipped into my office and said basically, "I can work *with* this person, but I couldn't work *for* this person." When I asked one of these people what the problem was, I remember her words clearly. She said, "That guy has got more friends than he can *use*."

That was just it—he used people. He never thanked anybody. He never celebrated with anybody. He never went to lunch with anybody. He never developed friendships among his own sales team. He had a "do it because it's your job" attitude. He never shared the credit. He was the Lone Ranger of selling.

If I promoted him, I would have lost four or five of the best technical sales reps. He basically capped out his career because he was not a team leader.

I usually hear from him only every few years—whenever he's looking for a job.

The everyday give-and-take of little exchanges is known as *reciprocity*. It is the currency of social capital. As Harvey Mackay says in the title of his book, *Dig Your Well Before You're Thirsty.*[16]

Performance

Nothing promotes success like success. People who perform tend to build influence. Their ideas get listened to a little bit better. But if salespeople point to the numbers and say, "Look at my numbers, this makes my ideas right," when the numbers aren't there, nobody listens to them anymore. Powerful people build on multiple sources of power.

Jack Nicklaus was the most competent golfer on the tour early in his career. But many disliked him, not only because he was beating a charismatic hero, Arnold Palmer, but because Jack was inelegant and ineloquent. That is, until Mark McCormack, the famous sports management figure, encouraged him to get a charisma transplant. Now he still makes more money than anyone on the tour even though his playing has waned with age. Michael Jordan, on the other hand, mastered task and personality, charisma and competence, early in his career and can sell ten-dollar sneakers for 110 dollars.

Common Goals, Common Enemy

Common goals or common ideology—these are the things that unite different groups into alliances. A contemporary example is Netscape, America Online, and Sun collaborating against the common enemy of Microsoft. Americans teamed with the Russians against Germany, and then later with Germany against the Russians.

People can be influenced to do what you want if you can show how it gets them what they want. Common goals, enemies, and ideology can unite religious groups, political parties, companies, and even countries.

Ideas and Innovations

When you want to think outside the box, there are some people we always want because they are always creative thinkers. One of our principals, Joe Terry, used to work for me as a sales rep in Texas as part of our government business unit. There was also a vice president of that business unit. But if a meeting was scheduled, everybody would want Joe there; we didn't care whether the vice president of the business unit could make it because Joe had all the ideas.

And he built influence. He knew this marketplace was different and why. He had performed well—he had sold more than anybody else. He had developed a group of supporters within the company. He had executive presence and a good sense of humor. When meetings were scheduled, he had what's known as "calendar dominance." People would schedule the meeting around his calendar because he had the best ideas.

Money

There are benign uses of money for influence, there are dark uses, and there are gray uses. Benign uses of money for influence include the biggest donor to a charity, the biggest stockholder, the banker who's toting the note, and the biggest customer.

The dark sources of influence include bribes and kickbacks, unethical, immoral, and illegal in some parts of the world, and a way of life in others. The gray area is perhaps the most insidious— political contributions, expediting fees, phony consulting arrangements, hiring consultants and law firms for access to government officials, and hiring ex-government officials to sell back into their own agencies.

Leadership, Salesmanship

Sometimes power belongs to those who seize it, who take the initiative, and who get out in front and lead until someone stops them. When our company was acquired by our major competitor's parent company, *our* chairman John Imlay was given control of the combined company instead of the chairman of our competitor. Why? Because John had built more influence with the competitor's management based on his leadership and sales ability.

Social

Other factors notwithstanding, people buy from people they like. Getting to know someone away from the office helps build those special relationships and can be very useful when the issue turns to business. Social influence includes activities like tennis and golf, clubs, schools, spouses, and friends. Professional associations and other executives in the same industry can be extremely influential. Some chairmen are more influenced by CEOs of other companies in the industry than by their own vice presidents.

If you don't think spouses can be influential, read *Barbarians at the Gate*.[17] The person behind the largest leverage buyout in history is Linda Robinson, wife of Jim Robinson, chairman of American Express, who was funding the management team's attempt to take over R.J. Reynolds. She is a New York businessperson and socialite who knows everybody. She was the catalyst that made the deal happen—seeing people at dinners and social gatherings and calling people on ski slopes. She got the right people together with the right messages but had no formal part in the process.

Charisma, Style, Presence

Personality, oratory, and persuasiveness are classic sources of influence. There are some people whose presence simply fills the room.

Some people are more fun to be around than others, and fun is a high-level personal value on Maslow's hierarchy. My brother Rusty has made his living that way. One of the funniest people around, he is half Johnny Carson, half Robin Williams. And he is competent at his job. He was vice president of stockholder relations for a major bank with a fire-breathing CEO in an environment where one word could cost a billion dollars. Had he not been good at his job, he couldn't have survived.

If all you've got is style but no substance, you can linger but you won't last.

Integrity, Dependability

If influence is social currency, then integrity is gold. People can move beyond influence and rapport to trust by knowing that you won't do anything to serve yourself at my expense. Sir Thomas More, Chancellor of England, was one of the most highly-respected people in medieval Europe. Henry VIII, who wanted another wife, was stuck for many years simply by More's silence because he would not approve the marriage to Anne Boleyn. More's respect came from the knowledge that he was the most principled man in the realm. This was a man who would die for his principles, and indeed he did.

Loyalty

Corporate loyalty has taken a beating in the last few years. With the scale of downsizings, reorganization, and mergers recently, it's hard to have loyalty to a company. Perhaps it never was possible. But you can be loyal to people, and they can be loyal to you wherever you are—as long as they have the power.

Some other sources of influence, both positive and negative, legal and illegal, include:

- Tenure, seniority
- Mentors
- Persuasiveness, oratory
- Shared experiences
- Threats, intimidation, blackmail
- Control of resources
- Common friends
- Ethics, fairness
- Teams
- Previous work
- Experience
- Who hired whom
- Family
- Expertise, competence
- Dependability
- Fame, fun, humor
- Vision
- Tradition, culture
- Connections
- Information
- Credentials

The ethical means of building influence are the building blocks of a relationship, of trust, of a career. Theodore Levitt, in *Thinking About Management*, says it well:

"Trust and reputation are not discretionary. They have always been necessary for doing business, and increasingly so as those who deal with each other are strangers and live distantly from each other.

"They are as necessary in business as the people in whom they reside. In no way is this more obvious than in the many activities and elaborate rituals that characterize the relations between business buyer and business seller.

"Often they appear casually social, convivially involving play, food, drink, and spouses. In fact they are anything but casual. The rituals are fixed and taken seriously by their participants.

"Their purposes are clear but unspoken—to test one another's veracity, reliability, and trustworthiness, to create and reciprocate obligations of performance, and to ascertain via close observance in casual settings the extent to which claims and promises that cannot be tested in advance can be relied upon, lest terrible consequences follow later."

Authority and Influence

We've defined influence as the ability to get things done without the use of authority. There can be people with authority and no influence, people who have influence and no authority, people with both, and people with neither.

People who have authority without influence have plenty of time to see salespeople (probably because no one else is talking to them). This scenario can be caused by poor performance, the Peter Principle (people rise to their level of incompetence), changes in corporate culture, mergers and acquisitions, or integrity problems.

There are many titles for this type of person, such as vice president of special projects or vice chairman. In Germany they call them "breakfast directors." In Japan, they are known as "the people at the window" because the people with the influence are actually on the inside of the building and lifetime employees who have lost influence are on the outside. This has confused many American salespeople as to where the real power lies. In Texas, these people are called "big hat, no cattle."

People with influence and no authority, however, can be extremely powerful agents and important to unlocking the complex sale. These include rising stars, executive assistants, secretaries, and technical experts, especially those who can link technical issues to the strategic issues of upper executives of their organizations.

We build emotional bank accounts with each other.

Stephen R. Covey
The Seven Habits of Highly Effective People

Many of these influential people lie outside the buying organization altogether, such as consultants, lawyers, friends, professional associates, and—yes—salespeople. These influencers are essential to leveraging strategy in the complex sale for four reasons:

1. They provide access to top-level executives.
2. They link technical or operational issues to strategic and political benefits.
3. They provide information that is needed to win.
4. They lead other people who have neither influence nor authority but may be involved in the decision.

Power Maps

You need to begin mapping out the zones of influence from the first visit. In one-on-one conversations, slip in questions such as, "How long have you worked here? Where did you work before? What do you look for from this project? Who influences whom? Who else's opinions are important to this decision? Who has whose ear? To whom do people listen in this organization? Who else might become involved in this decision?"

Obviously, political information is best handled discretely in one-on-one conversations out of earshot. Sometimes you need to cut someone out of the pack, or isolate them, so there are no witnesses to the conversation. This is why we entertain—so we can discuss politics and personal agendas in private.

As we said earlier, we have written about the six keys sequentially, but in reality we pursue the opportunity by using them *simultaneously*. You find the *pain* or *gain* and *qualify the prospect*. You then create early *preference* for your solution with the buyers who hold the most *power*. They will play major *parts in the decision-making process*. You may qualify out at any point where the chances of winning do not compare well to other opportunities.

Five of the keys are inputs that lead to the strategic sales *plan*. The plan is the sixth key in our process and the payoff of the analysis. If you are a single salesperson, the result is clear commitment about what tasks are necessary to win and how to spend your time most productively. If you are leading a team, the plan empowers each member to execute his or her part and effectively leverages efforts.

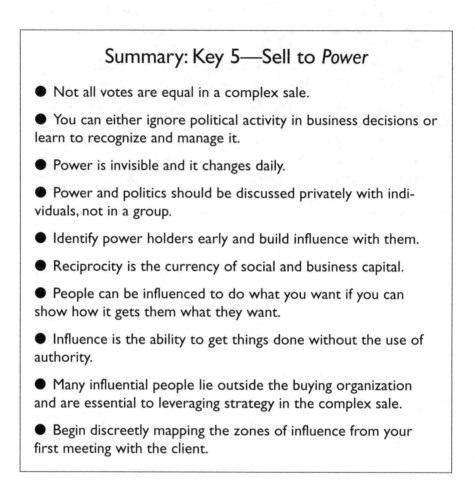

Summary: Key 5—Sell to *Power*

● Not all votes are equal in a complex sale.

● You can either ignore political activity in business decisions or learn to recognize and manage it.

● Power is invisible and it changes daily.

● Power and politics should be discussed privately with individuals, not in a group.

● Identify power holders early and build influence with them.

● Reciprocity is the currency of social and business capital.

● People can be influenced to do what you want if you can show how it gets them what they want.

● Influence is the ability to get things done without the use of authority.

● Many influential people lie outside the buying organization and are essential to leveraging strategy in the complex sale.

● Begin discreetly mapping the zones of influence from your first meeting with the client.

For a set of wall posters containing the chapter summaries and quotes from this book— please contact: Nautilus Press, Inc., 4279 Roswell Road, Suite 102-282, Atlanta, GA 30342; info@nautiluspress.com; ph. 1-800-324-4582.

CHAPTER 12

Key 6—Communicate the Strategic *Plan*

Speed has become an important element of strategy.

Regis McKenna
The Regis Touch: New Marketing Strategies for Uncertain Times

Key Questions

■ *How do we plan to win?*

■ *What do we sell to whom, where, when?*

■ *Have we tested our plan?*

■ *Do our tactics support our strategy?*

■ *How could our plan fail?*

It's been said that some salespeople make things happen, some watch things happen, and some wonder what's happening. The difference lies in having a strategy and leading a team to execute it effectively.

Strategy is a plan to deploy resources in a way that brings your strength to bear on the opponent's weakness, creating momentum that leads to victory.

You can win without a strategy. It's called luck. Direct salespeople are paid to make their own luck. You can get luck with a Web site.

The models of strategy descend from (like it or not) military history. In the last few years, many business executives and military leaders have been studying classical leaders' strategic models to determine the models of strategy, which can be applied to company or marketing-level strategies of today.[18] We do this because the models are timeless; the application is situational. It requires allegorical thinking. Models allow us to anticipate future events and to communicate that vision. *Intuitive or "natural" salespeople or managers without mental models may have trouble leading a sales team because they don't know why they are good and can't transfer that knowledge to someone else.*

Classic historical strategy drives market strategy; market strategy drives industry or territory strategy. *At the sales level, it is critical we strategize at four different levels*: (1) the industry market level, (2) the enterprise level, (3) the opportunity level, and (4) the individual level. Each level requires different technique, talent, and technology that can communicate the enterprise strategic account plan worldwide.

In a strategy session in Singapore with a client that sells oil exploration systems, one of the salespeople was showing a plan for a presentation scheduled for the following Monday in Indonesia. During the forty-five-minute presentation, an expatriate who had just moved from London was sitting in the back of the room smiling.

At the end he said, "Nice presentation. But would you be interested in knowing what's been going on at corporate headquarters of this account for the last year?"

"Tell me," said the rep.

"We are two weeks away from a 2.5-million-dollar value pricing agreement with this company, the agreement has been negotiated by our chairman, and is going to the board of directors for approval. This deal is already done; you don't need to do this presentation on Monday at all.

"By the way, that empty spot in your organization chart is being filled by one of our sponsors who will be driving the implementation. All you can do is mess this deal up.

"Do you want to know how? If you quote one percentage more than twenty-percent discount, it will ruin the whole deal because our chairman has stood the line for months to get this kind of pricing for this volume. If you quote twenty-one, twenty-two, twenty-three, or more, you will discredit us all and ruin the deal."

What happened here is not unusual. An individual rep doing opportunity-level activity was ignorant of enterprise-level strategy. This happens all the time and is a major obstacle to large account management. Even worse, at many companies with poor account management programs and poor commission or revenue-split policies, individual sales reps not only fail to cooperate on deals but actually fight among themselves. They look like several different companies to the client. One Big Five firm unknowingly underbid itself for the same engagement by two-thirds of the price, which not only left money on the table but also left a year's supply of egg on one partner's face.

> We need to strategize at the industry level, the enterprise level, the opportunity level, and the individual level. Only then can you drive a complex sale strategy in its entirety.

Why Strategies Fail

> *Failures are divided into two classes—*
> *those who thought and never did,*
> *and those who did and never thought.*
>
> John Charles Salak

Knowledge is power; the more you know earlier, the more advantage you can have. It's amazing how little most business developers know about their accounts after months of involvement and considerable resources.

Failure is the seed of learning. By studying why strategies fail, we learn how to make them succeed.

One of the major reasons strategies fail is *poor information.* There is not a general out there who wouldn't trade troops for better knowledge of where the enemy is and which way they're headed. That's why spies are so important. In the Persian Gulf War, our initial strikes were to knock out the information and command centers and blind the opposition.

Another reason for strategic failure is *no strategy* at all. Imagine a quarterback in American football coming out on the field and having a huddle. The team asks what the play is and he says, "I don't know, let's just go for it." (We've all been in *those* presentations.) If the quarterback calls the snap and fades back to pass and the rest of the team is going out for an end run, this person is going to get footprints all over his body. Effective power comes when the entire team knows the plan and can execute it, with timing, together.

Some salespeople have a clear strategy, but they keep it in their head. They *don't communicate the plan to the team.* This makes empowerment impossible if people don't know the goals and objectives in the plan. Napoleon used to ask the front-line officers to see if his plan had come down the chain of command the way he intended.

Another fatal error is *not having a plan B.* Some leaders plan only for the best possible outcome and assume how the competition will react. They don't test their plan and develop alternatives. The speed of change in marketing and sales today is so fast that a rigid, inflexible, or static plan will result in defeat.

Speed of information drives speed of strategy drives competitive advantage. By the time you win an opportunity, you may be on plan D, E, or F. This doesn't mean we should be indecisive. *There must be a conscious reanalysis and coaching process for absorbing new information and processing it into new strategies, tactics, and actions.*

In World War II, the Japanese were very good at plan A. They were elaborate detail planners, and things would work as long as everything went according to plan. But in the fog of war, things would change. They were not good at processing new information and coming up with a new plan.

In the naval battle of Midway, thirty minutes of indecision and delay in reassessing strategy cost them four aircraft carriers to the allies' one. General Slim, a British general in Burma, used the metaphor of a hill full of ants—very organized until you kicked it, then it became confused and took a long time to get reorganized.

Adolf Hitler had dual strategies without clear priorities when he attacked Russia, creating two fronts. When he waffled in the attack on Moscow, he cost himself two weeks and was caught by the Russian winter.

The best salespeople and the best generals are continuously thinking of alternate plans, while staying decisively committed until new information arises.

Other sources of failure include *poor execution*. Patton said a good plan violently executed beats a perfect plan we're constantly thinking about. He also realized that speed gives the opponent less time to perfect their plan and defenses.

Strategies also fail because of *bad timing*—the right thing done at the wrong time, too late, too little, or even too early. Because issues and politics change, a time-based strategy is essential to victory.

The inability to have a process for absorbing new information and generating new accurate strategies can often lead to *indecision*, *poor priorities*, or *waffling*, all of which can prove fatal. IBM's response to the justice department's attempt to break them up resulted in not two but three strategies that were not a migration path for the client but were competing strategies, leading their decline in the 1980s.

A classic principle of strategy is not to divide your forces in the face of a superior foe—*spreading yourself too thin*. Multiple strategies *can* work. The allies did it successfully in World War II. But it requires more resources, clear priorities, and decisive leadership.

Failure to pursue a victory was detrimental to the Union in the early parts of the American Civil War. General George McClellan was notorious for failing to follow up victories.

In sales, this translates to winning the opportunity and not driving that first sale to account dominance.

The last source of strategic failure in sales is *failure to pursue the battle won*. "Hit-and-run selling" or "drive-by selling" is when you get inside the walls, then leave for the next opportunity rather than selling from the inside out.

The best account managers use opportunity management in tandem with account strategy. Why? Because real profitability comes from shorter sales cycles and better margins on repeat business after you gained access, built trust, and reduced risk.

A Dynamic Strategic Planning Model

The following standard strategic model is one that could be used to write a business plan for a new venture, develop a business plan for a division, or manage any particular project. The model is neither new nor hard to understand; its execution and speed of revalidation are the challenges.

Dynamic Strategic Plan Model

Figure 12-1 *This is a traditional strategic planning model. The important thing to observe about our version is that it is a dynamic loop. It is a cyclical process of reassessing information and revalidating the objective. Goals that are quantified and date-driven are objectives. Our strategy is our approach and the tactics are the dynamic action items to achieve it. Critical testing of our own plan by the team avoids assumptions. Execution often yields new information that starts the revalidation cycle anew.*

Patton said, "Luck favors the man in motion." By this he meant that the person in motion not only keeps his or her opponent off balance and unable to process new strategies but in the process of action, he or she finds out more information faster than the enemy.

It is a mistake to look too far ahead.
Only one link of the chain of destiny can
be handled at a time.

Winston Churchill

This information processing cycle is known by fighter pilots; they live and die by it. In the movie *Top Gun*, Kelly McGillis asks Tom Cruise, "What were you thinking up there?" His reply was, "You don't have time to think. You take time to think up there, you're dead." By that he meant it must be habit and reflex. The pilot must have all the models in his head to be able to process strategy instantaneously.

Many salespeople don't process this at all. They pick a company and product strategy and plod straight ahead until they either win or lose. If you could always win on company and product, why do you need salespeople? Most salespeople don't know when to trigger alternative strategies. Those who do, win more often.

Those who are victorious plan effectively
and change decisively.

Sun Tzu
The Art of War

Dynamic, Flexible Strategy

The first step in the strategic process is *information*. The more we know—about the competition, the decision-making process, the politics, and the client's needs—the better we will be able to formulate a more accurate strategy.

Information drives strategy. Then you need a *vision of victory*. Salespeople need a mental picture and map of how they plan to win. They also need electronic communication tools to get it out of their head and into the teams' heads. Then the team needs effective presentation skills and graphics tools to get the benefits out of their heads and into the prospects' heads.

Next, you need to set *goals* and *objectives*. These terms get switched around semantically, but a goal is more general than an objective. An objective defines what you want to do in measurable quantities and is date-driven. It is less important what you call it than that you have one and execute it well.

Setting a clear objective is essential to defining the strategy. If we don't know where we're going, any road will do. Covey says, "Start with the end in mind."

Strategy is how you intend to achieve the objective; it's your plan of attack. It is how you plan to allocate resources, what you're going to sell to whom, where, and when. *Tactics* are the day-to-day detail actions you do to execute the longer-term strategy.

Strategy Coaching Reviews— The Antidote for "Happy Ears"

The most essential part of a strategic plan is the *testing* of it. Professor Tom Kosnik of Stanford University says, " Testing their strategy is what separates the amateur strategists from the effective ones." But it's also where our tradition of positive mental attitude can get in the way. The best of plans require critical thinking and that is perceived by some people as negative.

It is true there is a self-fulfilling effect of positive thinking. However, too often this results in assumptions, or "happy ears," for salespeople who are always ignoring the facts. The account looks good, right up until it's lost. There is a balance point of critical thinking, attacking our own plan without becoming negative. In the movie *A Bridge Too Far*

Bad news early is good news.

about Montgomery's failed attack at Arnhem, the Polish general Sosabowski (played by Gene Hackman) said, "But what about the Germans?" No one wanted to question the assumptions in the plan, and the attack failed.

One thing is certain: Your plan will be tested—by the competition, the client, or Murphy's laws. But it *will* get tested. Salespeople who were too busy to plan will now have to find another prospect.

Bad news early is good news because we can either refine our strategy or withdraw from the account. Blind spots late are bad news. Bill Gates says about himself in *Business @ the Speed of Thought*, "I have a natural instinct for hunting down grim news. If it's out there, I want to know about it." "An essential quality of a good manager is a determination to deal with any kind of bad news head on, to seek it out rather than to deny it." A *Fortune* magazine article on "Why CEOs Fail" describes one of the warning signs of executive denial as a background in sales or marketing.[19]

Who do you want to test it? Your own team. And from whom do you want the bad news? People who want you to win—your own team. But it means leaving your ego at the door and improving your plan rather than defending it. Testing plans on the job is *learning by losing*—a far more expensive approach, except for the fact that lost sales never hit the books, so you may never know how bad you really are.

For every self-fulfilling positive mental attitude success story, there are a dozen disasters in sales and marketing from people who didn't adequately challenge their own plan. Edward DeBono has a book called *The Six Hats of Thinking*. One of these is a red hat for the positive thinking aspect, but there is also a black hat where we attack our own plan to find the flaws in it before the competition does.[20]

> When do you want the bad news? From whom do you want it?

Nothing increases positive mental attitude more than winning. If we can anticipate the failure points and strengthen them, we should have a much better plan as well as plan B, C, and D in the pocket.

Next, you must *execute*. The devil is in the details. But an average plan can be overcome by great execution. Likewise, a perfect plan can be defeated by poor execution.

Finally, you get *results* and *new information* based on a call, a presentation, or a survey. In sales it is essential that you process new information and come up with a new plan or revalidate the old one.

The best time to reevaluate strategy is right after a sales call (not in the elevator or the bathroom, but after we get out of the building—the walls have ears). The curbside review is important to detect new information, critique performance, and make sure who has the ball on each action item. If you scatter like quail for the airport without taking this valuable time to strategize, you have missed a great opportunity.

The next time to revalidate your plan is in a strategy session before each major event requiring resources—the big proposal, the big presentation, or the corporate visit. These are essential. Once your top executives say the wrong thing because they weren't prepared adequately, you can't buy enough "mind erasers" to get it out of the prospect's head. "What the chairman *meant* to say our strategy was—never mind."

Coaching—The Manager's Value Added

Competitive advantage doesn't come from *awareness* of a strategy; it comes from *consistent execution faster* than the competition. Coaching is where managers can make the difference. And yet many sales managers and most consulting partners don't see this as a major part of their job. They simply "flog the forecast until morale improves." Salespeople need more than "how much and when?" from their manager.

Pipeline reviews by management in a coaching environment are where you drill down into the competition's strategy, the value proposition, and the politics of the decision-making process. More accurate forecasts come from a foundation of better sales plans for accounts controlled early and reviewed often.

Strategy and Tactics

When it comes to strategic planning, tactics should fall out of the strategy. But too many salespeople go "ready, fire, aim." Abraham Lincoln said, "If I had nine hours to chop down a tree, I'd spend the first six sharpening my ax." Many salespeople are out there chopping with a dull ax, generating tons of paper and lots of sales activity without felling any trees. But salespeople don't get paid to be busy; they get paid to win. It's been said that tactics are doing the thing right and strategy is being sure we're doing the right thing.

Tactics are short-term and flexible; they change dynamically. Strategies, however, should stay consistent until new information is introduced and you have made a conscious decision to commit to a new strategy. Both strategies and tactics are essential to success; a plan will fail for lack of either.

Tactics in the absence of a strategy creates a dependence on luck. General Bedel Smith, Dwight Eisenhower's chief of staff, said, "Luck is where preparation meets opportunity." Great salespeople, like great generals and athletes, make their own luck. Hannibal, the Carthaginian general who crossed the Alps to defeat the Romans, said, "We will either find a way or make one."

There are multiple strategies that *could* win. Looking for the perfect one will cause the loss of valuable time. Commit to one decisively, execute it violently, and revalidate it constantly.

The terms "strategy" and "tactics" often get confused, and the reason is that they are actually "nested." An action item can be *both* a strategy and a tactic at the same time, depending on the level from which it's viewed. What is a tactic to the enterprise becomes a strategy for the lower division. What is a tactic for the division becomes a strategy for the department. So the same item, viewed from above or below, could be either a strategy or a tactic. It's less important what you call it, than that you write it down and do it.

Now that you've been introduced to the six keys to understanding the complex sale, let's take a look at how to apply them to specific sales situations. We'll give you sixteen opportunity-level strategies and how to deploy them.

Sustaining advantage requires continuous improvement and change, not a static solution in which strategy can be set and forgotten.

Michael Porter

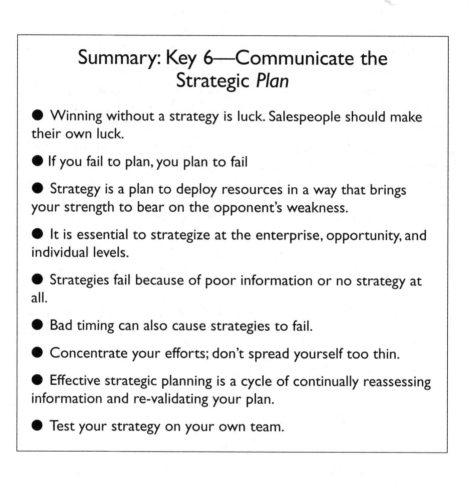

Summary: Key 6—Communicate the Strategic *Plan*

● Winning without a strategy is luck. Salespeople should make their own luck.

● If you fail to plan, you plan to fail

● Strategy is a plan to deploy resources in a way that brings your strength to bear on the opponent's weakness.

● It is essential to strategize at the enterprise, opportunity, and individual levels.

● Strategies fail because of poor information or no strategy at all.

● Bad timing can also cause strategies to fail.

● Concentrate your efforts; don't spread yourself too thin.

● Effective strategic planning is a cycle of continually reassessing information and re-validating your plan.

● Test your strategy on your own team.

For a set of wall posters containing the chapter summaries and quotes from this book—please contact: Nautilus Press, Inc., 4279 Roswell Road, Suite 102-282, Atlanta, GA 30342; info@nautiluspress.com; ph. 1-800-324-4582.

Strategies for Execution

CHAPTER 13

Sixteen Opportunity-Level Sales Strategies

> *A good way to outline a strategy is to ask yourself: "How and where am I going to commit my resources?" Your answer constitutes your strategy.*
>
> R. Henry Miglione
> *An MBO Approach to Long-Range Planning*

Key Questions

- ■ *How will we deploy resources?*
- ■ *How will we defeat the competition?*
- ■ *How will we gain a commitment?*

Sales strategy should fall out of marketing strategy, and marketing strategy is usually a model of historical military strategy. (That's the reason for the military examples in the book, which have been put in call-outs for those who appreciate them—and for those who don't.)

Merely categorizing or naming a plan doesn't make it a strategy. We have defined sixteen *specific* sales strategies that fall into five traditional categories. The general categories are groupings or attributes of strategies rather than strategies themselves. Within each group are strategies that illustrate the essential elements of a sales strategy—*what to sell to whom, when.*

Preemptive Strategies

The first type of sales strategies are preemptive—winning the battle before it starts.

One approach is to **demand creation rather than demand reaction.** Sometimes the best lead is no lead. This is especially true if it is in an account where we already have a presence.

If account management is done well enough, opportunity management isn't needed because we either gain first rights of refusal, preferred vendor status, or at least a chance to influence the requirements. Once a lead is received, the competition is also aware and the race is on.

Another way to win preemptively is to **ask for and seek an exclusive or sole source evaluation.** This obviously has a better chance of working with satisfied clients, but some vendors never set this as an objective. "Mr. or Ms. Prospect, why don't you evaluate our system, which is a leader, against your needs? If we can meet those needs, then you can gain months in time-to-benefit by shortening the evaluation and moving on to a solution.

"Your people will have a sense of participation by evaluating our system against their needs, and if they find it doesn't fit, you can always expand the evaluation later. In return, we'll pass on the savings in marketing costs in the form of an exclusive evaluation discount." (Even when you lose here, you win. Later on, when they begin the commodification process and ask for price concessions, you can remind them of when you asked them to take a discount in return for a shorter sales cycle and they refused. If price wasn't important then, is it really important now?)

An effective preemptive strategy is to **align yourself with a power partner.** Some software firms join forces with the consulting firm that also has the audit relationship. These people often have access to power and a strategic partnership relationship with the client. Aligning yourself with a power partner could effectively win the battle before it starts. Having a broader solution may also allow you to flank your opponent to other departments with capabilities that they don't offer.

Another preemptive strategy is to **walk away early,** especially where you think the decision-making process isn't fair or doesn't allow you to demonstrate your strengths. You weren't going to win anyway, but you may get them to change their process to give you a fair chance. Sometimes you can walk away and still stay. If you are a major player, this may shock the executives into reexamining the project team's decision-making process to see if it's a level playing field.

Use of this strategy is also a function of how many opportunities you have in your pipeline. Late in the game, this strategy doesn't work and is perceived as being a poor loser. They will simply wave goodbye to you. But early in the game, when they need you to build consensus and for due diligence, it could allow you to walk away and stay at the same time.

Obviously, walking away as a strategy is easier if a salesperson has a full pipeline of opportunities from which to choose.

Frontal Strategies

The next strategies are frontal strategies, the old direct assault. But this only works when you have superiority. In ancient military times, it meant three-to-one superiority because the enemy could fire and reload that many times before soldiers could cross the battlefield. Of course, these numbers changed during the American Civil War and World War I with the development of the rifled barrel and the machine gun. The technology had exceeded the tactics and generals had no new strategies.

The same thing happens in selling. Many a resource is wasted because salespeople plod ahead blindly with company and product, either because they don't know what else to do or they don't have an early detection system to tell them when it's time for plan B.

Sell the Product or Proposal, Sell the Company Story

You can get away with frontal or direct strategies if the client can easily perceive that you have a superior product and company. You can dash to the demo and leave the benefits linking to the client.

When a competitor gets relative demo parity, however, you must realize you have skipped the first two steps in the sales cycle—the requirements definition and the needs assessment. If your killer demo doesn't work anymore, you can't then go back and say, "Excuse me, can we understand your needs more fully?" You can't put the scrambled eggs back in the shell or the toothpaste back in the tube.

> *If the only tool you have is a hammer,*
> *you treat everything like a nail.*
>
> Abraham Maslow

Frontal strategies work in selling when you have product or company superiority. If you've got a killer of a category as in Geoffrey Moore's *Inside the Tornado*, don't try to outsmart yourself; show that product as often and as early as possible to as many prospects as possible.[21]

Doug Adams was the first nontechnical, professional salesperson to be hired by a major provider of optical equipment known for its high quality. At his first sales meeting he watched the experienced technicians outline their convoluted flowcharts of the sales cycle. At the end, they handed the marker to Doug, the newcomer. He went to the board and wrote:

1. Demo

2. Close

After the laughter subsided, he went on to sell twenty-eight machines that year compared to the previous high of six. He knew he had product superiority and a single decision maker, the physician. Why make it harder than it needed to be? He has since risen to become an industry-networked consultant (INC) and now buys and sell healthcare *companies*.

The direct approach worked for IBM when it introduced its personal computer line. Heavy advertising and the Big Blue label and distribution channels gained it dominant share until Dell outflanked it by going around the distribution channel via the Internet. As the PC became a commodity, Dell moved with the market and made it easier to buy.

Flanking Strategies

The second group of strategies are flanking strategies, bringing strength against weakness. This requires innovation, speed, and surprise.

To decisively move from plan A to plan B, the question that must be cycling in the salesperson's head at all times is, "If they had to decide today, who would win?" If the answer is "not me," it might be time for plan B.

Traditional flanking or indirect movement is a way to bring one's strength against the enemy's weakness, the weakness being the end of their line.

> In a flanking move, even though you have a smaller force, all you have to do is raise your sights to cover the enemy's entire line with enfilading fire while only the soldiers on the end can fire at you. This is how Sergeant York captured 132 soldiers single-handedly in a trench in World War I.
>
> If you can get behind the enemy and cut off their line of retreat and communication and supply, you can create a sense of panic and rout the entire force as Douglas McArthur did at Inchon. Stonewall Jackson did it at Chancellorsville, and Norman Schwarzkopf did it in the Persian Gulf war.
>
> Flanking in marketing or sales includes changing or expanding the issues, altering the buying process, or introducing new players to your advantage.

At the marketing level, Miller created a flanking strategy with Lite beer in the American beer market. American Airlines did it with frequent flyers, although it only gained them about six months' advantage. Lee Iacocca at Chrysler did it when it changed the marketing message from engineering excellence to warranties, rebates, and minivans. *USA Today* changed the publishing industry with an easy-to-read national newspaper. Ted Turner and TBS created an end run around the U.S. television networks through TV satellite feeds to cable programmers. Had he gone directly against the American networks, he would have been unsuccessful.

Turner did it again with CNN. Fred Smith outflanked the trucking companies with Federal Express. He wrote a paper in college saying that the most efficient way to ship a package from San Francisco to Los Angeles is through Memphis. I think he got a C on the paper.

Many of the greatest innovators in marketing today are college dropouts. This is because they don't teach this skill in college. The greatest marketing campaigns are the ones that haven't been thought of yet, so how can you teach this type of creativity?

From a sales point of view, someone once wrote that flanking strategies meant changing the ground rules. This is a simple solution to a complex problem. Flanking strategies in sales situations actually mean one of five things: (1) changing the *pain*, (2) changing the *power*, (3) changing the *process*, (4) linking *solutions* or *products*, or (5) expanding *scope*.

Changing the pain means either finding *new issues* to link into, linking into higher issues that have not been connected before, or linking them to issues that are sponsored by more powerful people. It may also mean refocusing the client onto the more important issues.

Changing the power means either encouraging your sponsors to exert their power or bringing in *potential influencers* who have not been drawn into the evaluation yet.

Changing the process means adding steps or taking out steps that would allow you to demonstrate your strengths or expose the competitor's weaknesses.

Linking solutions or products, or integration, is one of the benefits that separates a solution from a product. If you can link your solution technologically or economically into the client's current products or processes, they will benefit from lower risk and the simplicity and leverage of dealing with fewer vendors. Linking into a business partner's products may yield an easier, more integrated solution to the buyer and a competitive advantage to the seller.

Expanding scope means broadening the proposal (or the client's requirements) to include products or capabilities the competition can't deliver as well or at all. One of our clients, SAP, sells large integrated enterprise systems. A favorite strategy is to broaden the evaluation to include the entire spectrum of their products. Because of their breadth and integration of their offering, *they have a better chance of winning a big deal than a small one.*

A North Carolina bank client with our human resources system was evaluating a fixed assets system. The meeting, which was to be held the following day, seemed like a dead heat. I was sitting in Atlanta asking myself the question, "If they had to decide today, would it be me?"

I had no indication that I was winning, and since I don't like fifty-fifty odds, I assumed I must be losing. I called the VP of human resources and said, "I know what you want—those two additional modules to your system that you'd like to get. They're not large enough to discount by themselves, but down the hall they're evaluating another system. If I could put all those on the same contract, it would be more than one hundred thousand dollars, and I could discount them all fifteen percent.

"Let's see—you get your system cheaper, they get their system cheaper, and you get to deal with one vendor. How does that sound to you?"

"It sounds like a winner to me," he said.

"Do you know the chief financial officer?" I asked. "I can't get to him because I'm blocked by the project team. Shame on me, but that's the way it is."

He said, "Certainly. We're both outsiders at this family-run bank. We play golf together, and I know him fairly well."

"Could you go and suggest this solution to him? Oh, by the way, it has to be done by noon tomorrow, because the meeting is at two o'clock. At three o'clock, this dog won't hunt."

At four o'clock the next day, I got the call: We won. Did I leave fifteen percent on the table? Perhaps we would have won anyway. But would you take eight-five percent of a sure thing on a product that has a forty-percent margin? I believe so.

What did we do? We changed the power. We drew in a potential influencer that was not on the radar screen of our competitor. We also changed the pain from functionality to finance. We understood the decision-making process and that the strategy must be executed before two o'clock the next day.

During a sale to Turner Broadcasting, a pipeline review revealed we were losing at the project team level. We decided to search for and attempt flanking strategies. I met with the consulting firm that was our auditor and the client's consultant.

The result was a meeting with the consulting partner. During the lunch, I said, "I don't get good feelings about this account. If they had to make a decision today, who would they pick?"

His response was, "Well, I've been out of town for a couple of weeks. I'm not sure where the project stands."

"But if they had to decide today, who would you think they would pick?"

"I don't know, it's too close to call."

I didn't need to ask him the third time. He had already told me twice it wasn't me. In journalism, this is called a nondenial. He had two opportunities to give me a clue that I was winning, both of which he avoided. If I don't know I'm winning, I must be losing, or at least that's the way you bet.

So I said, "What can we do to turn this around?" He laughed because he knew I had broken the code.

He said, "Rick, if you knew the account (Ouch!), you'd know they have no cash. They need systems for the new computer they got with the acquisition of MGM. They're a leveraged buyout. They've borrowed a billion dollars to make these acquisitions. Every penny they've got goes for interest payments. Have you got any way they can buy with no cash?"

I said, "Well, cash is kind of near and dear to our heart, but what do you have in mind?"

"Well, I don't know—installment payments, slash the price, leasing, barter?"

"Hmm, barter." I happened to remember that we had taken a deal from ESPN in the days when we owned Peachtree Software.

"Well, it's risky, but it's been done," I said. "Who can you get me to see?"

"I can get you in to meet the vice president of information technology and the chief financial officer." I was there the next day.

"Barter is kind of an unusual practice for us," I said, "but what have you got to trade?"

I was looking at a hundred percent of zero at this point. Believe it or not, the first thing they wanted to offer was a warehouse full of those bamboo steamers and ginsu knives they advertise on TV.

I laughed and said, "If I took 750,000 dollars' worth of ginsu knives, my chairman would use the first one on me. What else have you got to offer?"

"Well, TV air time, obviously."

Our response was that we had sold our retail division, we had a direct sales force, there were only a certain number of decision makers in our market, and we called on them directly. TV really wasn't a viable alternative for our type of system.

After trying to trade TV air time and even Atlanta Braves tickets, we found a solution. They suggested, "Airline tickets."

"Now, that's currency to me. I have a million-dollar line item in my region for airline tickets. Which airlines?"

"British Caledonia."

Not good. "I don't suppose they fly to Jackson, Mississippi. How about Delta tickets? We fly often with Delta. Delta tickets are cash to me. You can buy all you want for Delta tickets."

"Well, Delta pays cash to us, too," they said, "but I think we could work something out." So we structured the deal for a certain amount in cash and the bulk in barter to be done in any one of these media within three years.

On the way out the door, I did a couple of other things. I told them, "I don't want you taking this to the competition to whip-saw our proposal back and forth. I've got to go sell this to my management, we all live in the same town, and our chairmen know each other. So I need a gentleman's agreement that you're not going to take our proposal and use it to drive down the competition." Then I told the salesperson to expedite this contract.

Why did we throw up this smokescreen and accelerate the process? We wanted the competition in the dark, thinking they were winning as long as possible.

If I were my competitor, how would I defeat me? You might get the project team agitated because they've been doing an evaluation while someone else was upstairs working out a financial deal. It could create a palace revolt by the people who must implement the system.

Or the competitor might come in and say, "Me, too, we'll take barter as well." (They might even take the ginsu knives.)

Even though we put up a smokescreen, the competition did find out with about a day to go. They went to their management and said, "We were winning and now we're losing. What can we do? Our competitor has this barter deal. How can we respond?" Their chief financial officer said, "You can take barter, but we only pay half commissions," to which the sales rep responded by cutting the price in half.

What was wrong with this strategy? It still didn't link into the pain. The pain was *cash, not pricing*, and their proposal at half price took more cash than ours.

What strategies happened here? We changed the pain from functionality to finance. We were upstairs negotiating a strategic financial solution while the project team was downstairs looking at demos. We also changed the power. We got access to two top executives and were able to link into their issues. Finally, we changed the process by accelerating the decision-making process while we were winning to give our competitor less time to react.

Fractional Strategy
*Divide and Conquer; Penetrate and Radiate;
If You Can't Get a Loaf, Get a Slice*

At the enterprise level, this could involve getting a toehold piece of business, getting inside the door, and getting your hall passes so you can move to sell from the inside out. It also may mean isolating your opponents inside the account so they don't oppose you.

From a marketing point of view, Wang in data processing had virtually no chance going head to head against IBM. So they carved off the niche of word processing. "Why use your mainframe for word processing? Use our workstations." And they were very successful for many years.

Historic examples include Napoleon Bonaparte at Austerlitz and especially Admiral Horatio Nelson at Trafalgar. At Trafalgar, the battle was won on the admiral's ship the night before the battle. It was won with the plan.

In 1805, Napoleon was trying to invade England and had to defeat the British Navy in order to do that. Nelson, having the smaller force, knew he couldn't win the traditional way—ship to ship. So his plan was dramatic and innovative. Instead of lining up side by side, he sailed right between the two forces, the Spanish and the French.

For a while, the enemy's strength bears on Nelson's weakness, the front of his line. But as he crosses the T and the guns point out the side, suddenly the numbers change; all of his guns could bear on the enemy, and he raked their line. But even more important, at the same time in the battle, all the ships turned in the same direction, south, upwind. This created a two-to-one advantage of the British over the lower part of the line. The top half of the opposing force was downwind and had to turn around and tack back upwind, which took an hour. When they arrived on the scene, the British were already victorious.

How did the entire British line know to turn at the same time? Signal flags. The British had invented the semaphore a few years before.

This classic example shows the power of a strategy well communicated to a team and executed with timing, resulting in concentration of force, momentum, and victory.

Wal-Mart used this strategy to gain a foothold on K-mart. They picked the area where K-mart was weak—rural areas—and once they gained strength, they went at them in the cities and have dominated. Microsoft did the same thing to IBM. "You take the very important strategic piece of hardware. We want this little insignificant thing called the operating system." Now the tail wags the dog.

Another fractional strategy is a **partnering strategy,** where companies team up to present an entire solution. One company gives up the services, or a piece of technology, or a piece of functionality, and partners with another to present an entire solution to a client. Systems integrators use this strategy effectively.

A divisional strategy of **penetrate and radiate** is key for major accounts on a global basis. You must first gain a toehold, then move from division to division. Later, you may change your strategy to frontal and go in at the corporate headquarters to gain full deployment as their standard.

Strategy for Selling to the Government

Divisional is the approach for selling to government entities in that the first piece of business is usually dominated by procurement rules. It is very competitive and price sensitive, and you must win on price, product, or proposal to get your toe in the door. Once inside, however, you can reduce political risk by superior performance, link engagements together, use your hall passes to navigate to other opportunities from the inside out, and make your profitability on opportunities two, three, and four.

You must be committed to it with adequate resources that know the process or you need to get out. Repetitive outside-in selling to the government on price and proposal is a prescription for failure.

Timing Strategies
Delay or Accelerate

Time-based strategies involve slowing down or speeding up the plan to your advantage. If you are winning, it is to your advantage to **accelerate** the process and close the sale. There is no better defense than having the ink dried on the contract and money paid. Every day you are in a winning position and have no contract, you leave an opening for your competitor. To paraphrase American Express, "The contract—don't go home without it."

Russian retreats are ancient examples of delay or containment. They did it to Napoleon in Moscow in 1812 and again three times to Hitler in 1943. Churchill said, "Hitler must not study much history." The Vietnamese used this strategy against the United States in the Vietnam War. General Vo Nguyen Giap said, "For every one you lose, we will lose ten, but you will tire first." Other examples are the Alamo, Bastogne, and the Cold War.

From a sales point of view, delaying strategies means buying time until you can come up with either a frontal, flanking, or fractional strategy to win.

The last strategy is to *delay*. It's what you do to buy time when you're not winning. From a marketing point of view, the best at this was IBM in the eighties. They rarely had the best products first, but they could chill the market by preannouncing future products. Being a standards setter, they appealed to the strategic risk-reducing benefits of standardization, and people wouldn't buy anything from anybody until they saw IBM's entry. Now only Microsoft has this much power in the IT industry.

You can't win by delaying, and you shouldn't delay when you should be qualifying out. But it might buy you time if you can leak resources into the account while looking for a crack through which you can drive a truck. Raising risk issues is one way of buying time.

A friend of mine and now president of our firm, Brad Childress, used this strategy while selling to a telecommunications company, where we had lost the evaluation. He called the decision maker and said, "We're sorry we didn't earn your business. We know we had a superior solution, but evidently we weren't able to demonstrate it to you. By the way, what happens next?"

The client said, "We're negotiating with your competitor tomorrow."

Brad replied, "Well, you know, they made a lot of claims that we've never seen in the marketplace, so we're concerned. I hope you share that same concern. If you're negotiating with them tomorrow, would you mind if I offered you some things you might want to ask for in the contract?"

The project leader said, "I see no harm in that." Brad unloaded every snarling legal snake in the book: warranties, guarantees, deadlines, test periods, limitations of liability, and so forth.

Brad waited a day and called the prospect back and asked, "Did they flinch?" The client said, "Flinch? They flipped. They seem to be unwilling to put in writing what they claimed in the sales presentation."

"Can we talk?" said Brad.

The good news is, Brad won that deal. The bad news is, when we got the contract, it had every nasty, snarling legal snake in the book in it. But a competitor who is looking at one hundred percent of zero will take agreements they weren't going to take before. It took us about ninety days to clean up the contingencies on this contract and make it recognizable, but it went on to become a multimillion dollar strategic account. That was the toehold.

Delay buys time for other things to happen. People on the project team leave, priorities change, new players appear, acquisitions occur, competitors can stumble, or new capabilities are introduced—all of which beat passively losing.

Timing is the essence of strategy, and we have discussed it here in terms of accelerating or delaying the process to our advantage. Let's now move to one of the most advanced skills of strategic salespeople: how to use the changes in relative importance of buyer issues over a long sales cycle to time the changes in your strategy—selling the right things at the right time.

CHAPTER 14

Changing Issues and Time-Based Sales Tactics

Information is power.

Francis Bacon

Key Questions

- *What phase of the client's decision-making process are they in?*
- *What issues are important to them at what time?*
- *When can we change the issues to our favor?*

The dynamics of the competitive, comparative buying evaluation can become volatile. Often even the most experienced salespeople fail because they do the right thing at the wrong time. *The issues change in relative importance over a long sales cycle.* Consequently, sales strategies should be time-based, depending on the phase or stage of the sales cycle.

Some sales methodologies imply there is one perfect strategy that should not be changed. The history of strategy has proven this wrong in war, business, and sales. The speed with which you can refine or revalidate a dynamic plan is the key to victory. By the time a long sale is won, you will probably be on plan D, E, or F.

What causes things to become so topsy-turvy in the crucible? The issues change as the client approaches the decision-making phase of their selection process. If there is a tangible product involved, project teams feel they must analyze every technical aspect, looking for product fit against their requirements. But as they approach the decision-making phase and have found that several vendors have adequate solutions, the real issue that starts to rise is one of *risk*.

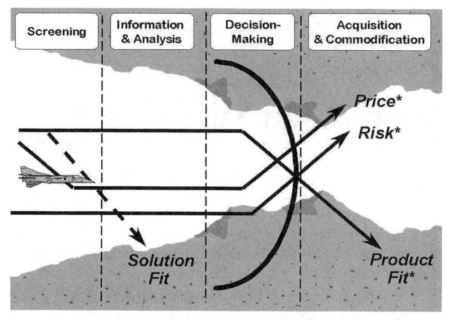

Changing Issues Require a Time-Based Sales Strategy

Figure 14-1 *This figure addresses how issues change in relative importance because of the typical phases of the buying committee process from their point of view. This means that the salesperson should emphasize the right benefits at the right time. It also defines the right time to change issues. Solutions providers don't spend as much time proving product function fit because they are perceived as having the services and resources to solve the problem.*

Risk Rises

As the client committee approaches a decision to purchase a solution, the difficulty of the post-sale implementation begins to rise as an issue. They ask themselves, "How are we going to install this? How are we going to implement it successfully? What processes must be changed along with the new product? How do we change work flows, compensation, performance requirements, and communication to create a successful solution?"

As the buyers approach the decision-making phase, issues can begin to shift off product features or solution fit onto implementation risk issues such as service, financial stability, responsiveness, references, and terms and conditions on the contract, such as penalty clauses, guarantees, warranties, delivery dates, and liquidated damages.

The bad news is that at this point the client is asking you all sorts of nasty, snarling legal questions. *The good news is that the client is asking you these nasty, snarling legal questions.* If after your capabilities presentation they are not asking you risk questions, they're not thinking about doing business with you.

At this point in the sale, the client is probably talking to one vendor about implementations and contracts and keeping the other two in the dark (but not telling them to go away). Those vendors in columns B and C are getting out-of-control signals—or silence. Or quite possibly the deal is not happening at all.

Price Is Resurrected

The other issue that starts to rise after the decision-making process is price. In the early phase of an evaluation, if you ask the client, "How important is price to your deliberations?" quite often you get answers like, "Not very," or "We want the best solution." In the middle of their evaluation phase they are preoccupied with functionality and requirements and capabilities. But at the end, it always comes back to price. The client, after their decision on a certain vendor, is now into their last phase, called acquisition, and a new set of games begins.

Commodification and Negotiation

It usually starts something like this: "Several firms can meet our needs, but your price is higher. What can you do about that? They all look alike to us. We can't tell the difference between any of them." This is called "convenient amnesia." It's a game buyers play.

After six months of studying the differences between the competing solutions, they now suddenly go blank and focus on price. Is it really because of the money? No. It's a sport. And if you can't pull out a list of differentiating advantages, then you're going unarmed into a battle of wits. If at that point you can't document your value proposition, you'll end up being commodified or discounting—or maybe losing altogether.

Where do these differentiating advantages come from? All the way back to the needs assessment or the requirements definition in the first place. That's where you understood the client's needs and where you found out if you had an advantage, if you qualified. And if you're headed into negotiation, you'd better take these items with you to document value.

In major sales of strategic items rather than commodity items, you must understand the real reason someone is asking for a discount or low price. Unless you are in a purchasing department, most business people are not measured on purchase price variance. Yet, they feel compelled at this point, as an agent of their company, to put on their negotiating hats with the vague idea they will gain some political points for having driven a hard bargain.

You must refocus them off the imagined political benefit that may come from a low price onto the longer-term benefits of the overall project. "Mr. or Ms. Prospect, how are you measured and what will you be remembered for three years from now—that you got a low price or that this project was successful? You'll ask for dozens of things not in the contract over the next few years. If this project goes well, the cost will be a detail. Besides, a lower price won't lower your risk; if the account is marginally profitable, it may actually increase it. If it goes poorly, no one will say, 'Well, at least we got a bargain.'"

Never go to purchasing or legal alone. Remember, these people would buy a pacemaker from the lowest bidder. Bargain with your sponsors early in the process when the price issue is not as important for them and ask them to accompany you to the negotiations.

The client's commodification strategy here is often to bring in a person who doesn't understand the value of what you are selling so he or she can play dumb to your selling value. Of course your sponsor at this point has to be an agent of their organization, but this person can explain the higher-level values and benefits and the reasonable risks associated with this product or solution. Otherwise you may find yourself arguing over thousands while trying to save them millions.

Product and Timing

Technical project team evaluators grind away on comparisons of features and capabilities early in the sale. Product detail can actually go away at certain times and under certain conditions. To show you how product fit can be minimized at the end of a sale, I'll share with you the story of a major sale to a cruise line in Miami.

The evaluation process was grueling. Two vendors were pitted against each other and were required to do detailed benchmark implementations in the evaluation of their products. It was an exhausting, detailed process with perhaps twelve to twenty people on each vendor's side.

In the end, we won by a couple of points, but we broadened that advantage into a business partnership. Their executives met our chairman. We had a corporate visit. We continued to talk about implementation and support and widened the gap. We actually reached a measure of business partnership before they signed the contract.

At dinner the night before the contract signing for multiple financial systems, the client said, "Oh, by the way, do you have a fixed asset system?"

"Certainly."

"How much is it?"

"Seventy-five thousand dollars."

"Add it to the proposal."

I thought, "They just bought a system sight unseen. How could they have required such detailed evaluation in the beginning and now they have bought a system they never even looked at?"

But they went even further.

They added the graphic user interface for all the systems, which they knew was in the prototype phase. There were no references for this three-hundred-thousand-dollar product at this time. The opportunity went from six hundred thousand dollars to almost a million dollars, and forty percent of it was on products they had never seen.

How could they evaluate in the beginning in such detail and buy products sight-unseen now?

The answer is trust. They trusted our products based on the ones they had evaluated. If those worked, then these must. They trusted us as a company because they had met our top executives, they'd been to our headquarters, and they knew we were a stable industry leader with a good track record of delivery. And they trusted us personally because we understood their business and we had become friends.

In addition, one of the political requirements in evaluation—involvement of the project team—had already been met by the exhausting detailed evaluation. It wasn't necessary to make them go through this again. They felt that they had been consulted, because one of the strategic things top management looks for by having these evaluations is involvement and buy-in from the project team. Nobody likes to have a system shoved down their throat, but we had already passed that phase.

When trust is established, evaluation cycles can fall to zero.

Products vs. Solutions

In that regard, positioning your company as a solutions company rather than a product or tools company can lower risk, increase trust, and shorten sales cycles. Andersen, Deloitte, and other major consulting firms don't spend eighty percent of their time proving product fit like product companies do. They sell a solution. They sell results. They'll make it fit, and they have the record and resources to prove it.

They'll either build it from scratch, integrate someone else's, or rebuild yours. The questions change to, "What do you want it to look like, how long will it take, and how much will it cost?"

What to Sell When

A time-based strategy tells the sales team when to sell which issues to whom. In the beginning of an evaluation the client weighs certain issues and considers them important, but later in the decision-making process their importance can change dramatically. Finally, in the acquisition phase a whole new set of requirements may evolve.

The savvy business developer recognizes these changing issues, takes advantage of this process, and capitalizes on it to shift issues to his or her own strengths. The sales rep without a dynamic strategy ends up a perpetual victim. The message is that what worked early in the sale may not work late in the sale and vice-versa.

Counterattacks

Opportunities don't coast across the finish line; they have to be pushed. Prepare for counterattacks at the end because nothing is more dangerous than a wounded competitor. A competitor that wakes up and realizes they are facing one hundred percent of zero will do things they weren't going to do before. They may raise new issues, they may go negative, they may try to go over the project team's head, or they may try to slash the price. A good competitive salesperson at this point must play defense as well as offense. They must anticipate these desperation tactics, predict them, and neutralize them.

We successfully held off a last-minute counterattack at the cruise line mentioned in the earlier story. Our competitor had an appointment for the following Monday, and we were trying to close the opportunity on the Friday before. We must have asked for the order a dozen times, but we were blocked. They kept explaining they had an appointment they felt obligated to keep next week.

We finally said, "We're ready to do business, and you're ready to do business with us. What else could they bring up at this point in the year, other than to try to stall it into next year or perhaps slash the price?

"Besides, if you're trying to be considerate, why don't you free them up to close a deal they can win at the end of the year? Why don't you call them now and ask what they're going to talk about Monday? If it's nothing significant, let's do business now."

The client thought about it for a couple of hours and called the competitor, and when they came back in the room, they said, "Well, just like you said, they tried to slash the price, and we told them we were not interested. We want to do business with you." When trust is established, price sensitivity goes down. Also by our preparing for the counterattack, their heavy price cut was seen as a desperation tactic rather than an attractive bargain.

Early Detection Allows Early Correction

Early information is the key to navigating the Death Valley sales cycle. *Speed and accuracy of information drive speed and accuracy of strategy, which drive competitive advantage.* If there is bad news, when do you want it? As early as possible, because then you can either change your strategy or sell somewhere else. Once the crucible is passed and the decision is announced, the cement is set. It takes a political jackhammer to change the shape of things now.

We've said that seeking bad news is not human nature. And doctors agree that the number one prevention of any illness is early detection. But most salespeople don't ask the tough questions because they don't want to spoil a perfectly good-looking forecast.

We now have a strategy to win at the opportunity level. What we now need are tactics to win peoples' hearts one at a time.

CHAPTER 15

Ten Individual-Level Strategies

A plan, like a tree, must have branches—if it is to bear fruit. A plan with a single aim is apt to prove a barren pole.

B. H. Liddell Hart
Strategy

Key Questions
- *"If they voted today, would we win?"*
- *"How do we get each person's vote or live without it?"*

Stakeholder Analysis

A *company* can't buy from you. *People* in a company or an organization do. People decide on a vendor as individuals before they decide as a committee. *Without a plan that takes our tactics to the individual stakeholder level, you have only given a name to your plan and called it a strategy.*

In the U.S. Congress one of the most important individuals is the Whip. The Whip's job is to count the votes and "persuade" enough holdouts to secure passage of the bill at hand. If there aren't enough to win, the vote is delayed, if possible. Very little happens by surprise.

Although salespeople don't have the same sanctions, they should use a similar process to assess your competitive position, drive strategy, and increase forecast accuracy.

Methodologies in the past have focused on competitive strategy only at the opportunity level. But nothing will drive a strategy to win better than a clear understanding of the decision-making process *at the stakeholder level*, person-by-person on the project team. (Whether we call an action a "strategy" or a "tactic" depends on the level from which it is viewed.)

The individual strategies and tactics by person, and the opportunity level strategy by competitor, will determine the sixth key to the complex sale, the *plan*, which must then be communicated to the team and revised as new information unfolds.

By this time, we have already qualified the *prospect* and are refining our plan. By analyzing each stakeholder using four of the keys, *pain, preference, power,* and *part* (in the *process*), we can arrive at the *individual-level* strategy and tactics of your strategic *plan*.

Illustration

Reynolds is a powerful supporter of ours; we have her *preference*. She is a decision maker and knows from her experience at a previous company that our solution solves her strategic business problem. She has *pain* and *power* and will play a major *part* in the decision-making *process*. Obviously, our individual plan for her is to (1) *support and motivate* her with whatever time and resources she needs to sell for us inside as she encounters obstacles. We must equip our sponsors with the business case and solution differentiators or preference will be perceived as cronyism based on politics alone.

Baker doesn't like us; he has negative *preference* for us. But his reasons are not connected to a major business problem but are based on a personal friendship with the competitor's rep. His organizational *power* is limited. Our strategy could be to (2) *disconnect* his opposition to us from the current major business *pain* and (3) *refocus* the others onto the company's issues and our ability to solve them.

Williamson and Biggs are supporters (*preference*) of ours from the previous engagement. They are vice presidents (*power*) but are not involved in the current evaluation—they have no part in the *process*. They may like us but that won't help unless they have a vote. Our plan is to show them how our solution affects their business problems (4) (*raise pain*) and (5) *encourage* them to get themselves added to the evaluation team as evaluators (6) (*change part*).

> I once had a group vice president fly across half the country to arrive unannounced and uninvited to inject himself into an evaluation team. He was too powerful to refuse, and he did it because his area was affected and he knew that based on experience at another firm, our solution was better.

Burns doesn't like us (*preference*) but it doesn't really matter. Burns is so disliked in his own organization (negative *power*) that nobody respects his opinion. His *part* is low, one of many recommendors, and his business problem (*pain*) is nonstrategic. We can afford to (7) *ignore* him. To alienate is never a strategy for anyone, but we don't need to spend much time here.

Leahy and Weldon prefer the other vendor—Leahy, a lot, and Weldon, a little. They are both respected C-level officers (*power*) and decision makers (*part*). Our strategy could be to try to (8) *change preference*, because if they voted now (*process*) we would lose. We could perhaps turn an objection to an advantage, clear up a misunderstanding, demonstrate a better vision or proof of our solution, link it into newfound pains, or expand our proposal to provide a win for them. If we can swing one of these two votes, we would win two of the three decision makers and (9) *outvote* the other. And Weldon is the one closest to the fence, so our efforts may be best focused on him first.

This is good old face-to-face persuasion, the tactical execution of our plan. We could also enlist the help of others who have influence over the holdouts, both inside and outside the company. In fact, the strategic consulting partner (*power*) needs our product to make his engagement successful (*pain*), and he and Weldon worked at the same accounting firm. He is a potential influencer (*part*) that the competition is not even talking to because he isn't on the official organization chart. If we could show him why it's in his interest (*change part, get involved*) to have our product, perhaps he or Reynolds could sway Weldon, who is closest to the fence (10)(*borrow influence*).

Note that to intentionally *alienate* is never a strategy. Not only is it unprofessional, it might motivate this opponent to help the competition or to sabotage the project, either here or at another organization.

Without Individual Tactics, a Plan Is a Strategy in Name Only

Each of these individual strategies is a tactic of a larger flanking opportunity strategy driven by the recognition that our frontal strategy to date would not win. If the answer to the question, "If they voted today, who would win?" is "Not me," then it's time for plan B, which beats sitting around and waiting for the answer.

As you approach the crucible of the decision you could change the pain, change the players, or change the process or parts of the individuals in your favor. By the way, how many accounts have you had for months and don't know this much about them?

By mapping out the relationships of power, you can navigate from person to person and leverage your investment of time. Nothing shortens sales cycles more than selling high. We must learn not only how to gain access to executives, but what to say when we get there.

CHAPTER 16

Selling at "C-Level"— Calling on Chief Executives and Political Navigation

---

When any organizational entity expands beyond twenty-one members, the real power will be in some smaller body.

C. Northcote Parkinson

Key Questions

■ *How can we gain access to chief executives (C-level)?*

■ *What is our point of entry into this account?*

■ *What do we say when we get there?*

■ *How do we get back?*

The principals in our firm, The Complex Sale, are all successful senior sales executives who collectively have made well over ten thousand executive sales calls during their careers and whose real world experience with our clients has yielded a number of best practices for selling at "C-level."

Outside-In and Bottom-Up—The Hard Road

The best way to avoid going over someone's head is to start there. Choosing your point of entry is an opportunity to gain better control early. Many veteran salespeople, tired of being blocked at the lower levels, jockey hard and fast to gain initial access at higher levels. It doesn't always work, but the benefits are enormous in greater control and shorter sales cycles.

Unfortunately, on the first piece of business with a company, this isn't always possible. We are often contacted by a project leader or someone who has been charged with sending requests for proposal to vendors. Their first words to a salesperson are, "Direct all your inquiries to me" often followed by, "I'm the decision maker."

To a salesperson, project leaders can be gatekeepers. And they are often covered in political glue. Once you touch them, you're stuck. One approach is not to touch them at all. They may be nice people and they may be instrumental to your sale, but they can limit your political navigation. Someone once told me, "Try not to take 'no' from someone who can't say 'yes.'"

Taking You Higher

Sometimes you have no choice but to start at the bottom or middle and work your way up. If you are to navigate to top executives, you have two choices. The first, which is going directly over someone's head, is sure to alienate the subordinate and has little chance of success.

Instead, you have to find a reason in the contact's interests to take you to their boss. Once a gatekeeper is on your side, he or she can be instrumental in helping you navigate higher—if you give them a reason that's on his or her agenda.

Why would someone take you to their boss?

● **Recognition and glory.** If they believe you have a solution that will be successful in their organization, they will get the credit for bringing you in. But they have to believe in you and your solution.

● **Secure resources.** They may need help to gain staff or budget to proceed.

● **Mitigate risk.** In case this project craters, they want to get their boss in the boat with them.

- **Project scope (lateral).** When projects become interdepartmental or international, managers usually need to be brought in to coordinate with other business units.

- **Project scope (strategic).** When issues go beyond operational and begin to affect organizational politics or strategy, project teams realize the need for management involvement.

- **My boss, your boss.** Equivalent rank meetings are important to provide insurance in high-risk projects. They can insure resources, continuity, quality oversight, and problem escalation. These meetings also have a status value, especially in Europe and Asia where class distinctions are still greater. If their boss won't meet with you, it's a sign they aren't thinking of doing business with you.

- **Bargain for access.** Trade for access while the client has something they need from you. While they need you in the game for due diligence, you can take requests for proposals, information, and demonstrations to bargain for access to executives. Later on, when they have your materials and you're not leading, you won't have anything with which to bargain.

- **You asked.** Perhaps the only reason someone hasn't taken you to the boss is because you've never asked!

I had been a regular caller on John, the head of systems, when I found out that our competitor had succeeded in getting all the way up to the executive vice president, and they were bragging they had won the business. I went back to my friend John and said, "If you want our system you need to help me. Can you get me to the accounting department?"

"Certainly, I can get you and the accounting people together."

I was dazed. I wondered why he hadn't done it before. Well, because I never *asked*. It's not the customer's job to sell themselves. It's not their job to be politically astute.

What I should have been asking myself is, "Who else should I be calling on to earn this business?" And "How will the decision be made?" I was in my comfort zone. I was selling to the sold. It's the course of least resistance.

When we got to the accounting department, we did an excellent job of linking our capabilities into their needs, creating a strong preference. As they approached the crucible what happened next was unbelievable. A power struggle broke out: The vice president of accounting resigned, the autocratic executive vice president was fired, and the head of IT was fired for misappropriation of programming resources for his own outside consulting firm.

A meeting of the new executives was held, and we got there first because this time we did ask. We made considerable progress in positioning our solution and won before the competition reacted. Without executive access it would have gone the other way.

In order to make things happen in the complex sale, we have *to get out of our comfort zone* and *into the power zone.*

Sponsorship—The Passport to Account Management

The best way to get access to an executive is through another executive or a trusted colleague. Executives are barraged every day with dozens of voice mails, e-mails, and phone messages. Many of these are nonbusiness calls or not important. However, the ones that get the most attention and credibility are the ones that they are expecting based on the recommendation of a colleague. I call it "transferred trust," or the friend of my friend is my friend.

Bottom-up selling is difficult enough, but the irony is that once salespeople get to executives they fail to leverage that relationship to its fullest potential. Many times salespeople get to an executive, close the sale, and then they aren't seen again until there's a problem. Quarterly incentives and short-term thinking often create a hit-and-run selling mentality. In California it's called "drive-by selling." And it represents a chasm between competitive selling and repetitive selling.

> In order to make things happen in the complex sale, we have to get out of our comfort zone and into the power zone.

The gateway (as well as the barrier) to repeat business and reference business is performance on the last sale. If we deliver on what we have sold and create a satisfied executive, this creates a neutron of customer satisfaction that can lead to another marketing molecule. Proactive sponsorship can then allow us to rise to an entirely different level of selling.

I had just finished a successful engagement with Andersen Consulting and asked the partner, "Who else should I be calling on in your firm?" He gave me the name of another partner. "I've been trying to get to him for the last six months, but I'll call him on Monday," I said. The partner I was talking to smiled and replied, "You know it doesn't work that way. I'll call him on Monday, you call him on Tuesday." I called him on Tuesday and had an appointment on Wednesday morning at eleven o'clock.

I remember the presentation well. We were just beginning my white board presentation when the phone rang at seven minutes past eleven. It was the partner's wife who wanted to go to lunch. The partner put his hand over the phone and said, "Rick, I talked to the other partner yesterday. He said this was a great program for our firm. Just tell me how much to budget and who to train."

The very idea, interrupting my presentation! Of course, the hard part was not continuing to talk because all you could do at this point is talk yourself out of a sale. The sale was done. In seven minutes. A project team would have taken seven weeks or seven months to reach a decision. Top-down selling is easier and faster if you know how.

Executive sponsorship allows us to move from bottom-up selling to top-down selling and to shorten sales cycles. When you enter an organization from the top you can learn the right issues, spend time with the right people, and avoid vendor abuse from project teams.

Other Points of Entry

Additional sources of executive sponsorship include professional associations, industry network contacts, previous customers, other divisions, and third-party channel partners.

Every satisfied client is a neutron that can bang into another marketing molecule releasing enormous energy and enthusiasm for you and your company. Of course, if your clients are unhappy with the results of what they bought, then the nuclear metaphor becomes one of toxic pollution and fallout as one bad reference cancels out half a dozen good ones. But then, only a handful of companies reward salespeople for customer satisfaction.

The Executive Sales Call
Strategic Literacy—Get on the Executive Bandwidth

Technical benefits are important to people who actually have to use your solution. But executives speak a different language. They buy strategic, political, cultural, and financial benefits. This means that you may have to give as many as two or three benefits for one capability if there are both groups in your meeting. "Because we can do this, it means this to you in the factory, it means this to you in the finance department, and it means this to you as the CEO."

Executives' issues often include:

● *Strategic.* Competitive advantage, customer satisfaction, mergers and acquisitions, stockholders, boards of directors, growth, government regulation, litigation, market share, company image
● *Political.* Stockholders, boards of directors, promotion, recognition, elections, unions, succession planning, taxpayers, stakeholders, environment, trade barriers, risk
● *Financial.* Return on investment, cash flow, stock price, budgets, survival, economy, earnings per share, productivity, exchange rates, significant cost savings, third-party payments
● *Cultural.* Competitiveness, deregulation, innovation, quality, risk-taking, teamwork, communication, cooperation, vision, consensus

Executives have no shortage of pains. Link your product, technology, or solution into one of these issues, and you'll be broadcasting on their wavelength. Executives want partners who can help them run their companies better rather than carriers of products. This means new challenges to salespeople to become industry experts not just product experts. The business developer of today must see the client through the executives' eyes and learn their "stay-awake" issues. They must move the buyer-seller relationship up from coexistence to collaborative to co-management if they are to gain the inside track on the competition.

Building strategic literacy means reading and learning our client's business as well or better than they know it themselves. Research should be done both inside with internal supporters and outside through third parties and the Internet. Then we must sell strategic benefits to strategic buyers.

We have seen many situations where the sales team was on the wrong wavelength with the buyers. My friend Tom McNeight was presenting a financial system in a high-powered organization in the financial district of New York. His team was demonstrating proudly to an executive vice president the graphic user interface of their computer system and its ease of use for data entry.

After a few minutes, the executive leaned back, recoiled from the keyboard and actually said, "Terminal, schmerminal. Do I look like a data entry clerk at United Airlines? I don't care about ease of use. I'm never going to touch it!"

What happened here? They had been selling technical benefits to a strategic buyer.

There are strategic benefits to a better-looking graphic user interface for a computer system: employee productivity, employee morale, shorter learning curves, and training dollars. If it's a customer information system, strategic benefits could include customer satisfaction and competitive advantage. But those weren't the benefits they had emphasized here—and with disastrous results. As one of our clients, Madeline Ossit, said, "Selling technical benefits to strategic buyers is like dogs watching TV—they sit there and they nod, but you know they can't possibly be understanding any of it."

Connecting your capabilities or features to the higher level benefits will give you greater power in the sale. Here is an example of turning a small functionality advantage into a major sale by linking into the strategic issues.

One of our clients was selling a suite of financial systems to a water utility of a major Western city. Among the only capabilities she had that the competitor didn't was a small system for project tracking, which tracks the costs involved with construction projects—not exactly mission-critical. And yet her ability to connect this capability to strategic issues gave her the competitive advantage.

What in the world could be the connection between a project tracking accounting system and strategic issues of a water utility? If you know the financial culture of water utilities, they are regulated monopolies. They must go to a regulatory board of citizens each year with their cost figures in order to justify charging any higher rates. At the same time, they work to actually keep their costs down to increase profitability.

This water utility was in high-growth mode. The salesperson understood the accounting laws enough to know that in constructing a building, if you can track your costs, you can begin depreciating it by phase rather than having to wait until the entire project is finished.

This means passing millions of dollars in depreciation expense along months sooner than waiting for the project to be completed, thereby justifying higher expenses while actually keeping no greater outlay of cash. It was a sixty-thousand-dollar module that gave her the competitive advantage to win a six-hundred-thousand dollar sale, and the return to the client was about six million dollars a year in increased profitability. The competitor's system was half her price, yet had less value.

What is strategic to a chief information officer is quite often tactical to a chief executive officer, the doctor, or the end user. Hardware, operating systems, and technology itself are strategic to CIOs, but they are tactical to chief executives and users. What is strategic to the hospital administrator focused on costs is tactical to the physician focused on patient outcomes.

The Executive Sales Call—What Won't Work

"Tell me about your company." Ask this question to a C-level executive and what they will probably tell you is where the exits are located. The talk-listen ratio, which we learned in consultative selling, shifts somewhat back to the salesperson in the executive sales call. The consultative research is still important—but it has to be done *before* you get to the executive.

> Selling technical benefits to executive buyers is like dogs watching TV; they may nod, but you know they're not really getting any of it.

You should still have an interactive exchange with the executive, but if you've never met, you must establish knowledgeability of the company and the industry either directly or by referral. You can then go to reflexive listening and validating the executive's pain.

I took Nick Bradick of AMS to see my brother, then a senior VP with a major bank. After fifteen minutes of discussing bank and industry issues, my brother said to Nick, "Oh, I can see you're one of us." The relationship was transformed, and the sharing of information went up at that point because he knew Nick and his company could help the bank. He had earned insider status.

It took me nine months to work my way to Ray Lane, the COO of Oracle. With the help of five sponsors (especially John Keenan) inside the company and four outside, I was able to get a one-hour appointment. At the time he was reorganizing the company and temporarily had about twenty-five people reporting to him, so he didn't have time for discovery. I prepared eight hours with my sponsors for a one-hour call. It was an excellent exchange, and they have been a good client ever since.

The Outside Expert's Opinion— Benchmarks and Best Practices

They don't have time to tell you about their company; they want you to tell them something they *don't know* about their *own* company—with an outside expert's opinion.

"How do we compare to other companies in our industry? How do we compare to best practices and operating ratios?" Executives need an outside view of their firms because they get filtered information or stale thinking from their own people about the real status of their own firms.

Help Them Prepare for the Future— Ideas and Innovations

Executives are paid to set the strategy for their companies for the next five to ten years. And if the Peter Principle hasn't raised them to their next level of incompetence as they rose through their organizations, it is being thrust upon them from above. Changes in technology, globalization, competition, and deregulation are creating pains that executives have never faced before. They are looking for answers, and consultative salespeople are the harbingers of new solutions.

Create a Vision of Value

If the purpose of the call is to create demand, you will want to create a value proposition of the solution you propose and a vision of the pains that would happen if nothing were done. In this case, we are seeking a power sponsor to sell inside for us.

Some methodologies imply that a high return on investment (ROI) will naturally motivate buying activity. This assumes a logical approach to project sponsorship. Our experience has shown that unless your proposal has emotional and personal political benefits for the sponsor, nobody will take up the banner. Most chief financial officers have at least a half dozen proposals on their desk at any one time with sufficient returns on investment and not enough funds to do them all.

Motivating pain doesn't come from the rational side of the business problem; it comes if there is political recognition for success or embarrassment for inaction.

Why You? Differentiation

You not only need to show how you can do something better than the client can do for themselves, you must show why you are better than anyone else. Some capabilities or features are *satisfiers*—everybody has them. Some advantages are *absolute differentiators*—only you have them now. Others are *relative differentiators*—you do them faster, better, easier, or at less cost. A unique differentiator linked to an urgent strategic pain is the dream scenario for a consultative salesperson.

Seek Sponsorship

If you are successful at generating interest and need to work with others in the organization, be sure the executive sponsors you (rather than just refers you) to that individual with a phone call, e-mail, or personal introduction so trust is transferred effectively.

Get Your Return Ticket Punched

The challenge of an executive sales call is that you must create a reason to return or you will be on the outside again. If you have raised issues of value to the executive, work to define a reason to return—a follow-up to do, a question to research, a meeting at a future conference or trade show, a book or article, or a proposal. But it has to be meaningful. An unplanned call may mean you lose the access you worked so hard to gain. The worst thing you can do to executives is waste their time.

Winning Before the Battle— Account Management

CHAPTER 17

From Opportunity Management to Account Management

Key Questions

- *What is our overall plan for this account?*
- *Should we invest additional resources?*
- *How do we build company-to-company trust?*
- *Can we change their buying process?*
- *How can we earn preferred vendor status?*
- *Can we partner with this account?*

A friend of mine was an airborne instructor in the Army. I asked him if it was difficult to get people to jump out of an airplane the first time.

"Actually," he said, "it was harder to get them to do it the *second* time."

That is my definition of a great salesperson. Will they buy from you the *second* time?

If we oversold or underdelivered, then it wasn't a sale; it was a lie. Lying is easy; selling is hard.

A *great* salesperson sells in a way that leads to trust and repeat business.

One of the biggest challenges faced by sales management as market share grows is the transition to the next level of strategy from competitive selling to repetitive selling—from opportunity management to account management. Repetitive selling to existing clients is a different model that requires different strategies, talent, and rewards. In consulting, information technology, medical equipment, telecommunications, and finance, as well as many other industries, the integration of these two processes is vital to gaining profitable repeat business.

As mentioned previously, in some industries the buying decisions are committee evaluations; in other industries, such as consumer packaged goods, pharmaceuticals, or industrial supplies, account management means managing a continuous flow of goods or services.

To some firms account management means caretaking. To others it means appointing someone to fill out an account profile, list opportunities, and arrange executive lunches. To me it means creating demand, earning executive trust, and achieving a dominant market share within the account. It means ultimately *changing the buying process* to preferred vendor status or partnership and not having to compete as hard for repeat business.

Account management deserves its own volume, and it is addressed here only to the degree that it relates to this book. This chapter focuses on the differences and integration between periodic "event type" opportunity management and account management.

Investment Marketing

For project or event-type buying, account management is a process of *selling between the sales*—a concept that flies in the face of traditional qualification. There are considerable barriers to investing consistently in accounts that buy only periodically. Quotas, compensation plans, organizational boundaries, project delivery, quarterly focus of publicly-traded firms with high stock multiples, market share pressure, and the venture financing of firms with short technology half-lives—all are obstacles to long-term global account management.

Account management should drive opportunity management by influencing preferences, requirements, processes, players, and issues *before* an evaluation breaks out. But many companies consider them separate processes and fail to realize the enormous benefits of an integrated enterprise plan.

What is needed is a client life-cycle sales plan that is based on in-depth understanding of the client's business, on driving objectives, and on sharing and communicating tactics to the account team worldwide.

From the most effective practitioners of account management, we have defined an overall enterprise strategy of eight goals:

1. Penetrate
2. Demonstrate
3. Evaluate
4. Radiate

5. Collaborate
6. Elevate
7. Dominate
8. Inoculate

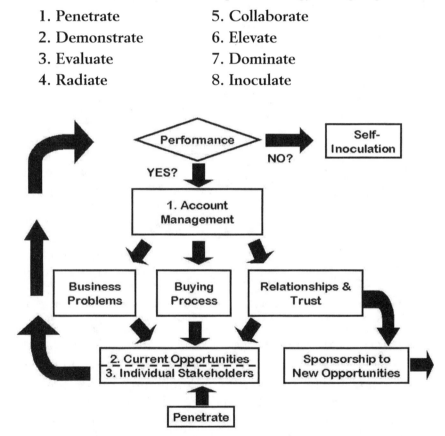

Figure 17-1 A proactive, integrated enterprise account plan requires strategy at four levels. After account penetration, performance on the first opportunity is the next hurdle to an account management model for selling repeat business. Failure to exceed expectations or document value delivered can poison the account for future business. However, earning the trust and reducing risk for powerful people can lead to a shorter buying process, referrals, or sponsorship to other executives throughout the enterprise or industry.

1. *Penetrate.* Penetration of an account occurs through either demand reaction or demand creation. Demand reaction occurs in response to an inquiry or request for proposal. The R.A.D.A.R.® process describes how to manage that approach.

Demand creation in a new account means gaining access to a power sponsor or someone who can take you to one, finding an emotional or political issue, and linking your solution to it. You must then support the efforts of your sponsor to sell your solution inside the organization. The higher your point of entry into the organization, the greater your chances of success.

Account Penetration
Points of Entry

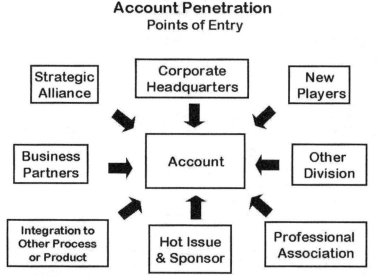

Figure 17-2 *The entry points used to penetrate an account are also the same that must be constantly defended. To inoculate your account from competitive intrusion, you must document value delivered and build preference for your firm, your solution, and yourself at each potential point of entry before the competition can gain a toehold. It must be an ongoing, proactive process.*

2. *Demonstrate.* The first hurdle in dominating an account is to demonstrate that you can meet and exceed client expectations for your products or solution. Make sure your performance has made your original sponsors look good for having selected you the last time. This means *documenting delivered value* and proactively claiming the benefits—both tangible and intangible—your solution has provided. Metrics and key performance indicators other than return on investment are required to measure the many benefits not identified readily by accounting systems.

3. *Evaluate.* Knowing which accounts to invest time and resources in is the challenge to both the sales manager and the individual account manager. Two of the most important factors are your own past performance and their culture. If they don't buy from anyone else on a partnership model, their culture toward vendors may be adversarial.

However, a customer may be a large account without being a partnership account. Getting high volumes without lower cost of sales or less competition may be worthwhile, but don't think it's a partnership. They're just high maintenance—but worth it.

The answer is to sell the way the customer buys, then allocate resources in that way. Thus, some accounts may warrant a team of dedicated resources and others only occasional calls. Beware that some companies will consume your attention and still treat you badly—it's in their culture. If you lavish partnership resources on commodity buyers, you'll partner yourself broke.

4. *Radiate.* Once a toehold has been established in an account, a proactive account strategy requires that you leverage the first engagement to navigate to the next. Otherwise you penetrate an account, go back outside, passively wait for the next proposal request, and remain a stranger to the account. Never put the soldiers back in the Trojan horse and go back outside the walls to wait.

Having delighted the client sponsors, the next step is to *initiate sponsorship* from one satisfied executive to another. Every satisfied executive is a neutron that can accelerate you to the next marketing molecule—to another department, to other divisions, to corporate headquarters, to other companies as sponsors move, or to industry trade organizations—releasing great energy for you. And by moving from one executive to another, you change your navigation *from bottom-up to top-down,* a far more efficient approach.

Likewise, if your performance is bad, toxic reputation spreads the same way, but you'll probably never know what didn't hit you. Failure to exceed expectations will mean that in the long run, you are actually performing a *sales prevention* activity and *inoculating the account* from further business with *you.*

The greatest internal barriers to radiating are a vendor's internal revenue recognition and revenue split policies, short-term goals and compensation, preference for the thrill of chasing new accounts, and lack of a proactive enterprise account plan and manager.

5 & 6. *Collaborate* and *elevate*. You must elevate two forces in the account to achieve dominance. We must elevate our value proposition up the value chain from operational commodity to strategically differentiated. We must also elevate our personal relationships from rapport to trust.

Moving to insider status means bringing in industry expertise to help your clients with *their* clients or constituencies. Collaboration could mean working with their design teams to co-develop new products or mission-critical systems specifically for their needs. It could mean working on joint marketing efforts or promotions. It could mean vendor-managed inventories for manufacturing, healthcare, or retail. It could mean cooperating on training or quality. Or it could result in integrating or outsourcing entire supply chain operations into virtual manufacturing parks that ship directly to the customer.

As this type of collaboration grows, personal risk is lowered and a new source of competitive advantage grows—your knowledge of their company and how to get things done in their organization. In some cases, such as enterprise-wide solutions, you may be instrumental in implementing massive changes in culture or process. Some of these new solutions are equivalent to betting the life of the company, and you are a consulting physician.

7. *Dominate.* To dominate does not mean manipulate. It means outperforming expectations and not giving anyone a reason to go to the competition. Delivering superior results and lowering risk creates *account inertia*—the tendency of an account to *stay* your account.

If your goal for an account is to be a preferred vendor or partner, then a new concept arises—*market share within the account.* How much of our type of product or service do they need and what is our current share? What share should be ours? You may be satisfied with what appears to be a large account to you until you measure how much potential really exists.

8. *Inoculate and Integrate.* Loyalty is a human emotion: an *account* cannot be loyal; *people* in the account can. That's why true client relationship management at the executive level is between people, not just computers. To develop immunity to competition, you need to develop individual loyalty to your company, your solutions, and you, personally, to the point that your allies serve as *listening posts* for competitive incursions or new players. They call you early so you can react to competitive intrusion.

How might the competition penetrate your account? From the same places you penetrate in the first place—new players, painful issues, integration from other processes and products, professional organizations, other divisions, or strategic alliances from the top.

To protect an account, you must proactively identify any potential decision maker for your products or services throughout the organization and build preference *before* the competition does. You must gain access, preferably through a sponsor, and document the value that your firm has delivered as well as your differentiations.

New players must be greeted at the door. Positioning, or the art of saying it first, is critical for newcomers. They may be carrying preferences for other firms, in which case you must *raise preference* for you and *document switching costs* to at least the point that they choose other battles to fight.

In addition, integrating systems, processes, design, training, and intellectual property increases delivered value, and makes switching costs higher. As relationships, processes, and cultures grow together, so does interdependence.

Gain the High Ground

In opportunity management, a lead is a good thing. In account management, a lead is a *bad* thing. A lead from within an existing account of ours means that a competitive evaluation is beginning and we didn't know it.

Market share does not equal customer loyalty. The trust of the powerful people in your account, both high and low in the organization, equals client loyalty. Your goal for these select accounts is to build such loyalty for your company, its solutions, and for you that the client never has reason to look elsewhere. We teach people to influence—to the degree possible—the politics, issues, competition, and decision-making process before an evaluation ever breaks out. It may have to go out to bid, but we want the high ground—not based on manipulation, but on earned trust.

Once the formal evaluation process begins, it's too late—the walls are up and the guards are out. Even your best clients may not talk to you. It's too late to be their best friend then.

When trust is established, sales cycle times can fall to zero. The highest level of trust is when the client feels that, "Whatever you're selling, I'm buying. Tell me what I need." The irony is that if account management is done well enough, you don't have to do opportunity management at all.

Abandoning adversarial or computer-dependent relationships and solving business problems collaboratively is a more productive buyer-seller relationship for those firms that sincerely practice it. If we can solve big problems and build company-to-company trust (there are however, limited partnerships with divisions or departments of large enterprises that are bigger than most other companies) we can achieve the following benefits:

- Demand creation
- Executive access
- Insider consultative status
- Less price sensitivity
- First rights of refusal
- Interdependency

The buyer benefits from lower risk, fewer vendors, greater leverage, and vendors who know how to solve problems in their company and who have the skin in the game of future business. Although lower-level personal partnerships abound in commerce and affect face-to-face selling, only executives with organizational power have the self-security and clout to deliver on the promise of shortening sales cycles for departments, divisions, or enterprises.

Despite the complexity of selling today's solutions, the secret is simple. It's about building relationships with the right people. Knowing their pain. Solving their problem. Earning their trust.

Aristotle said that relationships are based on three foundations: *logos*, *pathos*, and *ethos*. Competence, charisma, and character. It's what you do, who you know, and who you are.

In complex sales:

People buy from people—people with solutions.

Partners buy from people that they like and that they trust.

To be trusted, you must be trustworthy.

Are you that company?

Are you that person?

The Complex Sale, Inc.
3015 Windward Plaza • Suite 475 • Alpharetta, GA 30005
770.360.9299 • www.complexsale.com

Around the globe, in more than 50 countries, The Complex Sale teaches sales and business development teams the process and skills they need to achieve market differentiation and competitive advantage. The Complex Sale offers live account workshops that provide integrated process methodologies, a rich training curriculum and enabling tools as sophisticated as today's buyers.

- **R.A.D.A.R.—Competitive Opportunity Strategies** is a proven opportunity management methodology and live-account workshop that enables salespeople to better qualify and control the competitive, political sales evaluation. More comprehensive, yet easier for field reps to use than other methodologies, it gives your sales team a common language and strategic sales plan for winning the complex sale.
- **R.A.D.A.R. ® 1-2-3** is our web-based collaborative planning and communication tool for opportunity management that enables the principles and process of our methodology to produce a team sales plan.
- **T.otal E.nterprise A.ccount M.anagement®** is a sales methodology for helping sales forces build company-to-company relationships in strategic or global accounts, leading to improved customer satisfaction and significant repeat business.
- **PRISM®—Pre-emptive Integrated Sales Messaging** is for sales and marketing departments to develop powerful messages that link to strategic customer issues and enables you to differentiate your solutions effectively against your most significant competitors.
- **Bonfire of Management Principles - Creating A Winning Culture** is designed to turn new managers and top performers into winning managers. You'll learn how to build a common culture of principles, language and expectations among your management team.
- **BEARS – Beginning Engagements & Account Relationships Strategically™** can help you maximize revenue potential from your current client base.
- **Executive Demand Creation - Selling To Executives** will help your team deal with the sales process shift from "demand reaction" to "demand creation" selling by developing a process to penetrate an account through knowledge of and application to the pains of important people.
- **Sales Management Series: -Best Practices Sales Cycle & Coaching the Complex Sale** provides managers with a deeper understanding of the sales or business development process your firm is implementing, and their role as coaches.
- **Negotiating For Value Series: -Best Practices Negotiating Cycle & Negotiating For Value Workshop**
- **Consulting Solutions**

For a set of wall posters containing the chapter summaries and quotes from this book, please contact The Complex Sale at 770-360-9299 or www.complexsale.com.

NOTES

Chapter 2

[1] Michael Treacy and Fred Wiersema, *The Discipline of Market Leaders*, Perseus Books, 1995

Chapter 4

[2] Bill Gates, *Business @ the Speed of Thought*, Warner Books, 1999
[3] Neil Rackham, *Spin Selling*, McGraw-Hill, 1988

Chapter 5

[4] Michael E. Porter, *Competitive Advantage*, The Free Press, 1985

Chapter 6

[5] Stephen Covey, *The Seven Habits of Highly Effective People*, Simon & Schuster, 1989

Chapter 7

[6] Neil Rackham, *Spin Selling*, McGraw-Hill, 1988
[7] Abraham Maslow and Frederick Herzberg, described by Paul Hersey and Ken Blanchard, *Management of Organizational Behavior*, Prentice-Hall, 1969, pp. 57–62
[8] Noel Tichy, *Managing Change Strategically*, AMACOM, 1982

Chapter 8

[9] "Why CEOs Fail," *Fortune*, June 21, 1999, p. 69

Chapter 9

[10] Al Ries and Jack Trout, *Positioning: The Battle for Your Mind*, Warner Books, 1986
[11] Tom Peters, *Thriving on Chaos*, Alfred A. Knopf, 1988, p. 141

Chapter 10

[12] Thomas Bonoma, "Major Sales: Who Really Does the Buying?" *Harvard Business Review*, May-June 1982
[13] Robert Miller and Stephen Heiman, *Strategic Selling*, Warner Books, 1985

Chapter 11

[14] Henry Mintzberg, *Power In and Around Organizations*, Prentice-Hall, Inc., 1983, pp. 32–47
[15] Stephen Covey, *The Seven Habits of Highly Effective People*, Simon & Schuster, 1989
[16] Harvey Mackay, *Dig Your Well Before You're Thirsty*, Currency Doubleday, 1997
[17] Bryan Burrough and John Helyar, *Barbarians at the Gate*, HarperCollins, 1990

Chapter 12

[18] Al Ries and Jack Trout, *Marketing Warfare*, Plume (Penguin) Books, 1986
[19] "Why CEOs Fail," *Fortune*, June 21, 1999, p. 82
[20] Edward DeBono, *Six Thinking Hats*, Little, Brown and Company, 1985

Chapter 13

[21] Geoffrey Moore, *Inside the Tornado*, Harper Business, 1995

BIBLIOGRAPHY

*I have found in the course of my career, that
an awareness and study of people, history,
political issues, and social and technological
trends all lead to a better understanding of
the dynamics of the marketplace.*

Regis McKenna

Marketing

Levitt, Theodore. *The Marketing Imagination.* New York: The Free Press, 1986.

McKenna, Regis. *The Regis Touch: New Marketing Strategies for Uncertain Times.* Addison Wesley, 1986.

_____. *Relationship Marketing.* New York: Addison-Wesley Publishing Company, 1993.

Moore, Geoffery A. *Crossing the Chasm.* New York: Harper Business, 1995.

Moore, Geoffrey A. *Inside the Tornado.* New York: Harper Business, 1995.

Ries, Al and Jack Trout. *Marketing Warfare.* New York: McGraw-Hill, 1997.

Ries, Al and Jack Trout. *Positioning: The Battle for Your Mind.* New York: Warner Books, 1986.

Treacy, Micheal and Fred Wiersema, *The Discipline of Market Leaders.* Reading: Perseus Books, 1997.

Quality

Deming, W. Edwards. *Out of the Crisis.* Boston: MIT, 1986.

Peters, Thomas J. and Robert H.Waterman. Jr. *In Search of Excellence.* New York: Warner Books, 1988.

Peters, Tom. *Thriving on Chaos.* New York: Alfred A. Knopf, 1988.

Walton, Mary. *The Deming Management Method.* New York: The Putnam Publishing Group, 1986.

Personal Development

Ailes, Roger. *You Are the Message.* New York: Doubleday, 1996.

Carnegie, Dale. *How to Win Friends and Influence People.* New York: Simon & Schuster, 1981.

Covey, Stephen R. *The Seven Habits of Highly Effective People.* New York: Simon & Schuster, 1990.

DeBono, Edward. *Six Thinking Hats.* Little, Brown and Company, 1986.

Management and Leadership
Burrough, Bryan and John Helyar. *Barbarians at the Gate: The Fall of RJR Nabisco*. HarperCollins, 1991.

Gates, Bill. *Business @ the Speed of Thought*. New York: Warner Books, 1999.

Geneen, Harold. *Managing*. Doubleday, 1984.

Hammer, Michael and James Champy. *Re-engineering the Corporation*. New York: Harper Business, 1993.

Hersey, Dr. Paul. *The Situational Leader*. New York: Warner Books, 1985.

Kotter, John P. *Power and Influence*. New York: The Free Press, 1985.

Levitt, Theodore. *Thinking About Management*. The Free Press, 1991.

Miglione, R. Henry. *An MBO Approach to Long-Range Planning*. Prentice-Hall, 1983.

Maister, David H. *Managing the Professional Service Firm*. New York: Free Press, 1993.

Maxwell, John C. *The 21 Irrefutable Laws of Leadership*. Nashville: Thomas Nelson, 1998.

Oncken, William, Jr. *Managing Management Time*. New York: Prentice-Hall, 1984.

Selling
Bosworth, Michael T. *Solution Selling*. New York: Irwin Professional Publishing, 1995.

Dorsey, David. *The Force*. New York: Ballentine Books, 1995.

Hanan, Mack. *Consultative Selling*. New York: AMACOM, 1995.

Hanan, Mack. *Key Account Selling*. New York: AMACOM, 1993.

Imlay, John. *Jungle Rules*. New York: Penguin Books, 1996.

Miller, Robert B. and Stephen E. Heiman. *Strategic Selling*. New York: Warner Books, 1986.

Rackham, Neil. *SPIN Selling*. New York: McGraw-Hill Book Company, 1988.

Seibel, Thomas M. and Michael S. Malone. *Virtual Selling*. New York: Free Press, 1996,

Treacy, Michael and Fred Wiersema, *The Discipline of Market Leaders*. Perseus Books, 1995.

Wilson, Larry. *Changing the Game: The New Way to Sell*. New York: Simon & Schuster, 1987.

_____. *Stop Selling, Start Partnering*. New York. John Wiley & Sons, 1995.

Ziglar, Zig. *Ziglar on Selling*. Ballantine Books, 1991.

Strategy
Liddell Hart, B. H. *Strategy*. New York: Faber & Faber, 1967.

Ohmae, Kenichi. *The Mind of the Strategist*. New York: McGraw-Hill, 1991.

Porter, Michael E. *Competitive Advantage*. New York: Simon & Schuster, 1998.

Porter, Michael E. *Competitive Strategy*. New York: Simon & Schuster, 1998.

Tzu, Sun. *The Art of War*. New York: Buccaneer Books, 1996.

Politics and Influence
Cohen, Allan R. and David L. Bradford. *Influence Without Authority*. New York: John Wiley & Sons, 1991.

Handy, Charles. *Understanding Organizations*. Oxford: Oxford University Press, 1993.

Mackay, Harvey. *Swim With the Sharks (Without Being Eaten Alive)*. New York: Fawcett Book Group, 1996.

Mackay, Harvey. *Dig Your Well Before You're Thirsty*. New York: Doubleday, 1999.

Matthews, Christopher. *Hardball: How Politics is Played—Told By One Who Knows the Game*. New York: Perennial Library, 1989.

McCormack, Mark H. *What They Don't Teach You at Harvard Business School*. New York: Bantam Books, 1986.

Pfeffer, Jeffrey. *Managing with Power*. Boston: Harvard Business School Press, 1996.

Pfeffer, Jeffrey. *Power in Organizations*. New York: Harper Business, 1981.

INDEX